CHILDREN HEARING GOD'S VOICE

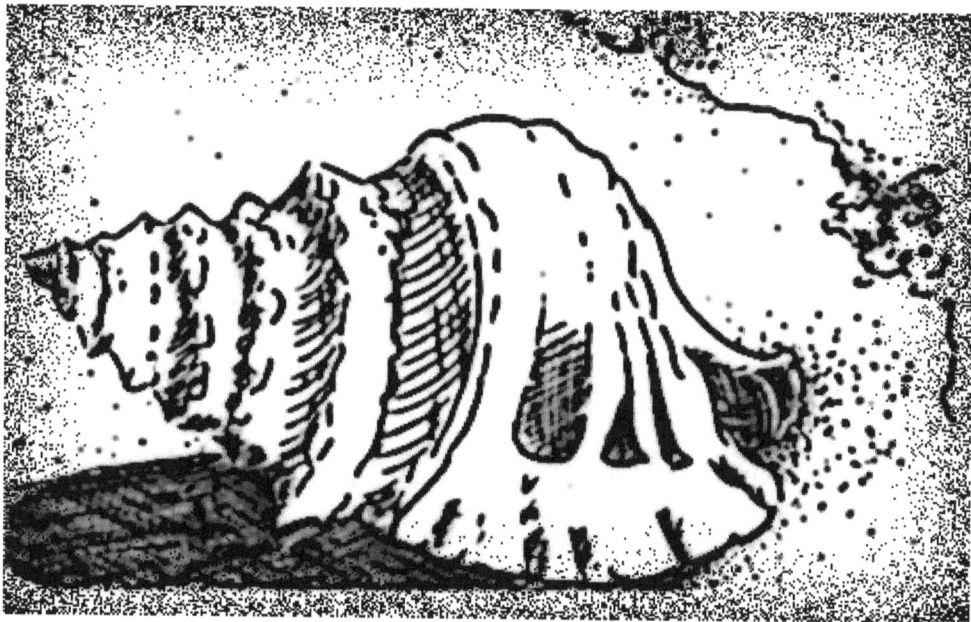

WORKBOOK

ZOE Ministries International

ZOE Ministries International
PO Box 2207
Arvada CO 80001-2207, USA
permissions@zoemin.org

Please see page 3 for permissible use of this copyrighted Workbook.

All scripture quotations, unless otherwise indicated, are taken from *The NIrV Adventure Bible®
for Early Readers, Revised*. Copyright © 2000, 2008, 2014 by Zonderkidz. Used by permission of
Zonderkidz. All rights reserved worldwide. www.zonderkidz.com

Thanks to colorluna.com for use of the Jesus Loves Me and the Other Children coloring page.

Thanks to The Church House Collection for permission to use The Hireling Fleeth coloring page.

Thanks to getcoloringpages.com for use of the Noah's Ark coloring page.

Thanks to biblekids.eu for use of the Disciples Find Jesus Praying coloring page.

Special thanks to Mackenzie Schmidt for her generous help by creating many illustrations in this Workbook. Mackenzie-studios.com

Special thanks to Brent Maiolo for sharing his beautiful sketches for the activities in this Workbook.

Rev. 01/20

PHOTOCOPYING AND DISTRIBUTION POLICY

The content in this Workbook is copyrighted material owned by ZOE Ministries International. Please do not reproduce content in emails or on websites.

For families: You may make as many photocopies of the Workbook pages as you need for use WITHIN YOUR OWN FAMILY ONLY. Photocopying the pages so that the Workbook can then be resold is a violation of copyright.

Schools and Co-ops MAY NOT PHOTOCOPY any portion of the Workbook. The best option is to purchase a Workbook for each student.

For ordering, go to our website www.zoeministries.org or call 303-673-9658.

CONTENTS

Dear children,

Jesus has a special place in His heart for His children of all ages. In the scripture below, He clearly says that the little children, like you, should come to Him.

"Some people brought little children to Jesus. They wanted him to place his hands on the children and pray for them. But the disciples told them not to do it.

Jesus said, 'Let the little children come to me. Don't keep them away. The kingdom of heaven belongs to people like them.' Jesus placed his hands on them to bless them…." Matthew 19:13-14.

WE BELIEVE YOU CAN LEARN TO HEAR THE VOICE OF GOD AND MINISTER TO ONE ANOTHER. We once heard of a Bible school that allows children to minister in a special way. When one of the teachers is sick, they bring in the small children to have them lay hands on and pray for him. Then God heals the teacher! Children are helpers who God can use for good. You can hear God's voice, you can have visions, and you can powerfully share what you know about Jesus—the King of Kings.

We pray that you, your family, and your friends will be blessed by what you learn from this training course. We also pray that you will hear God's voice more and more clearly as you grow. Visit the ZOE website for more information: www.zoeministries.org.

John 10:27 (NKJV) says, "My sheep hear My voice, and I know them, and they follow Me." THIS SCRIPTURE DOESN'T APPLY JUST TO ADULTS, BUT TO ALL OF GOD'S PEOPLE. Take this scripture, apply it during this training course, and watch the Lord work!

In Christ,

Dick and Ginny Chanda
Founding Directors

LESSON 1

THE BLESSING

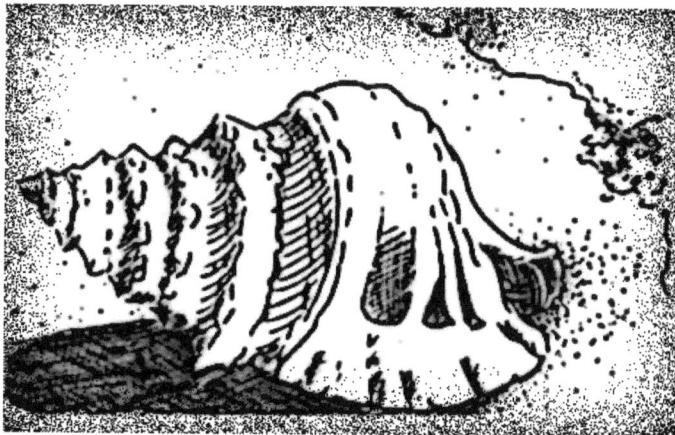

OBJECTIVE

Each one of us is valuable to God. He created each of us individually with a special purpose. God blesses us so that we can be a blessing to others.

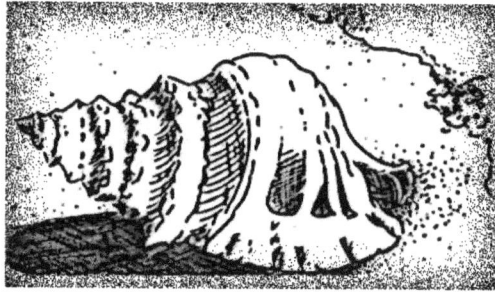

THE BLESSING

KEY SCRIPTURE

Mark 10:14-16 "'Let the little children come to me. Don't keep them away. God's kingdom belongs to people like them. What I'm about to tell you is true. Anyone who will not receive God's kingdom like a little child will never enter it.' And He took the children in His arms, put His hands on them and blessed them."

Or for younger children:

Mark 10:14, 16 "'Let the little children come to me...' And He took the children in His arms, put His hands on them and blessed them."

Copy the Key Scripture for this lesson in the space below.

READING THE BOOK

Read Chapters 1 and 2 in *Is That Really You, God?*
What in these chapters seemed interesting or important to you? Write out your thoughts.

MY NOTES ON THE TEACHING

LEARNING ACTIVITIES

Activity #1 God says I am good.

Write your name on the blank line in the verse Genesis 1:31a. Read the verse aloud with your name in it.

Genesis 1:31a "God saw everything that he had made. And it

[including _____]

was very good."

Activity #2 I am priceless to God.

Search YouTube for a lyric video of "Priceless" by For King and Country. After listening to the song "Priceless" a few times and reading the lyrics, copy the lyrics in the song "Priceless" that seem important to you.

What do you think God is saying to you through this song?

Activity #3 Before I arrived

God knew what you would be like before you were born. He is not surprised by who you are—what you look like, the personality you have, or what you like to do. Make a list of the people who were waiting for you to arrive.

_____   _____

_____   _____

_____   _____

_____   _____

_____   _____

Interview several people from your list, asking them the following questions:

Did you know anything about me before I arrived? If so, what?

Are you surprised by what I look like, the personality I have, or what I like to do?

Record the answers you were given below.

Activity #4 Make a fruit salad together.

Together, wash, cut up and combine several different fruits in a bowl. Each fruit is delicious and carries a vitamin or mineral to help us be healthy. Write below what you think God enjoys about you. What good things do you bring to your family and friends?

Activity #5 Your message to God

God invites us to call out to Him and He will listen to us. **Jeremiah 29:12-13 says, "Then you will call out to me. You will come and pray to me. And I will listen to you. When you look for me with all your heart, you will find me."** Write out something you want to say to God.

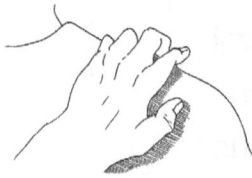

Activity #6 Jesus' blessing over you

If Jesus were right here with us, what would you like Him to say in a blessing over you? Write it out below.

Activity #7 God's blessing on His people

We know by reading the following verse what God wants for every child of His.

"May the Lord bless you and take good care of you. May the Lord smile on you and be gracious to you. May the Lord look on you with favor and give you peace" Numbers 6:24-26.

Write or draw what you think these verses mean.

Activity #8 Father Abraham

Galatians 3:7-9 reads, "…Those who have faith are children of Abraham…God said, 'All nations will be blessed because of you.' So those who depend on faith are blessed along with Abraham." So, if you have placed your faith in Jesus, you are a child of Abraham. Have fun singing along and following the actions to the song "Father Abraham" by searching YouTube for "Father Abraham Lyric & Dance Video."

Activity #9 Be a blessing.

Think of some ways that you could be a blessing to other people this week. Make a list of people you know and write what you could say or do to help each of them.

_____   _____

_____   _____

_____   _____

_____   _____

Pick one of these people and do or say something that would help him. Describe below what you did and what happened.

ART PROJECTS

Project #1 Make a creation ribbon.

Tracing the Lesson 1 pattern on the next page, make a Creation Ribbon. Write on it one of these phrases:
God's Special Creation or
Designed By God or
I Am Chosen.
If you would like, you could wear this ribbon.

Project #2 Jesus enjoys children.

Color in the coloring page on the next page that shows Jesus having fun with the children.

Project #3 Jesus blesses children.

Below draw a picture of Jesus blessing a child.

LESSON 2

JESUS IS OUR SHEPHERD

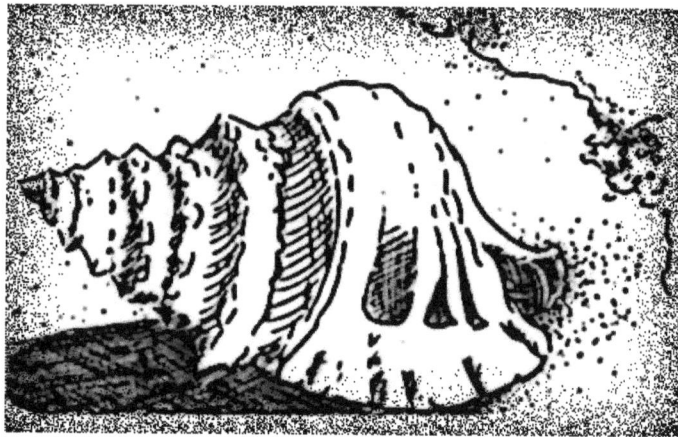

OBJECTIVE

*God is our Good Shepherd, and Jesus gave up
His life for us, His lambs. Like a shepherd, He
knows each one of us and wants to help us. One way He
does this is by speaking with us in our spirits so
that we can hear and follow Him.*

JESUS IS OUR SHEPHERD

KEY SCRIPTURE

John 10:14-15 "I am the good shepherd. I know my sheep, and my sheep know me…And I give my life for the sheep."

Copy the Key Scripture for this lesson in the space below.

READING THE BOOK

Read Chapters 3 and 4 in *Is That Really You, God?*

What in these chapters seemed interesting or important to you? Write out your thoughts.

MY NOTES ON THE TEACHING

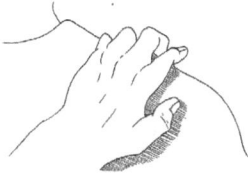

PRAYER AND MINISTRY TIME

When you think you have heard something from God that will encourage the person who will be prayed for this lesson, write what you heard below.

For instance, God may give you a verse from the Bible that will encourage that person. Or if God gives you a picture in your mind as you think about that person, ask God what the picture means. Then write what He says, or draw a picture of what you saw. Or God may give you a dream at night. If so, ask Him what it means for that person, and write it below. Share with that person what God gave you, and pray a prayer for him that is in line with what God gave you.

The person I am praying for this lesson is _____.

This is what God gave me for this person:

This is what I prayed:

Answer to prayer and date:

LEARNING ACTIVITIES

Activity #1 Act out the good shepherd and the hired hand parable.
Act out the parable of the good shepherd and the hired hand, choosing parts of the good shepherd, the hired hand, the sheep, and the wolf. Make props from construction paper and cardboard, and costumes from clothes you have. You could also just use one prop or piece of costume for each different character. OR you could make cardboard signs to tie around the neck, reading GOOD SHEPHERD, HIRED HAND, SHEEP and WOLF. Act out this story several times, changing parts.

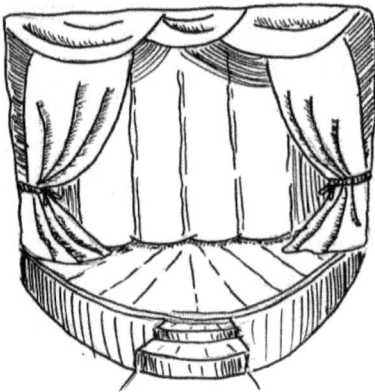

Activity #2 Tell the story.
Tell the story of the parable of the good shepherd and the hired hand. The story field can be made of a large circle of green paper. Using the Lesson 2 patterns at the end of your Workbook, trace the patterns on construction paper and cut out the shapes to create the different characters and props. Trace and cut out several branches from brown paper to build a sheepfold. Cut out large rock shapes from gray paper for the wolf to hide behind. Trace a wolf on black paper and cut it out. Trace several sheep on white paper and cut them out. Trace the shepherd and the hired hand patterns on different colored paper. Tell the story in your own words, moving the pieces over the story field. You may want to present this parable to a friend or relative.

Activity #3 David, the shepherd boy

Read **1 Samuel 17:32-37** to find out about King David when he was a shepherd boy. In the space below, write what you think about David. Was he a GOOD shepherd or not, and why?

Activity #4 Make a sheepfold.

Create a sheepfold out of sticks, cardboard or other materials. Sit or lay down inside, imagining you are a sheep inside it. In what ways does God protect you? List those ways here.

Activity #5 Illustration for Jesus' cleansing blood

With your parent's or teacher's help, re-create the illustration of Jesus for-giving your sin. Once you have practiced it, you could show this illustration to a friend or someone in your family.

Activity #6 Watch a video about Jesus washing away our sins.

Search YouTube for the video titled "A science experiment showing how Christ can wash away our sins" by Robert Nollkamper, and watch the video.

Activity #7 Read a true story.

What did you learn about God from the true story by Steve Lightle? Why did God wake up that man to talk to him? Ask your parent or teacher to read the story again, if it would help. Write your thoughts about this story below.

Activity #8 Watch a video about sheep and their shepherd.
Search YouTube for the video titled "Do sheep only obey their Master's voice?" by Øyvind Kleiveland. This is a video of a modern day shepherd whose flock will only come when he calls.

ART PROJECTS

Project #1 The Hireling Fleeth (The Hired Hand Runs Away) coloring page
Turn to the next page and color in the picture. What does this picture teach you?

Project #2 God took care of me.
Draw a picture of a time when God protected or took care of you.

John 10:13 The hireling fleeth, because he is an hireling, and careth not for the sheep.

Where is my shepherd?
Why do I get the feeling
that you are lying to me?

Let's be friends!

Church House Collection ©

LESSON 3

LISTEN, KNOW AND FOLLOW

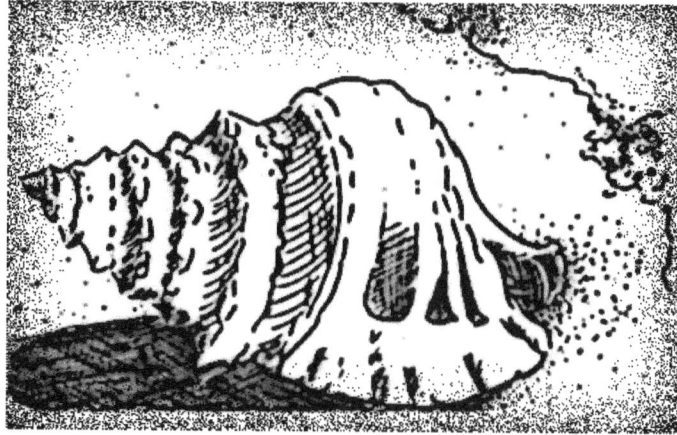

OBJECTIVE

Because we are children of God, we can learn how to listen, recognize and follow God's leading. We can recognize when God is speaking to us by comparing what we hear with what God has already spoken in the Bible.

LISTEN, KNOW AND FOLLOW

KEY SCRIPTURE

John 10:27 "My sheep listen to my voice, I know them, and they follow me."

Copy the Key Scripture for this lesson in the space below.

READING THE BOOK

Read Chapter 5 in *Is That Really You, God?*
What in this chapter seemed interesting or important to you? Write out your thoughts

MY NOTES ON THE TEACHING

PRAYER AND MINISTRY TIME

When you think you have heard something from God that will encourage the person who will be prayed for this lesson, write what you heard below.

For instance, God may give you a verse from the Bible that will encourage that person. Or if God gives you a picture in your mind as you think about that person, ask God what the picture means. Then write what He says, or draw a picture of what you saw. Or God may give you a dream at night. If so, ask Him what it means for that person, and write it below. Share with that person what God gave you, and pray a prayer for him that is in line with what God gave you.

The person I am praying for this lesson is _____.

This is what God gave me for this person:

This is what I prayed:

Answer to prayer and date:

LEARNING ACTIVITIES

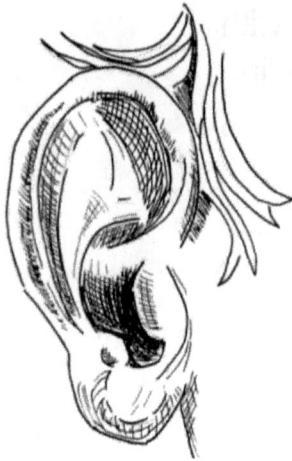

Activity #1 Ways to hear God more often and more clearly
Below are ways that we can better hear God speaking to us:

a. Talk to Jesus, praying either aloud or silently in your heart. Spend time listening. You can ask God a question and give Him time to answer you.

b. Read what God has already said in the Bible. As you read, see if the Holy Spirit makes a verse or passage stand out for you.

c. Write in a journal what you think He is saying to you. Sometimes He will speak as you write by giving you a thought.

d. Spend time singing worship songs, expressing your love for Him. He may speak to you during times of worship.

e. Spend time with other Christians by going to church and studying the Bible together. God may speak to you through them.

Have you heard from God through some of these ways? Which ones?

What new way would you like to try out?

Activity #2 Play "God Says" .

This game is like the game Simon Says. Only do what "God Says" to do.

Activity #3 Play "Guess Who".

When you were blindfolded and played Guess Who, was it easier to recognize the voice of a close friend or someone you do not know well? Write your answer below.

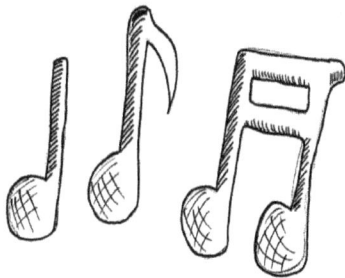

Activity #4 God is our good Father.

Search on YouTube for the song "Good, Good Father" by Chris Tomlin. Listen to the song and read the lyrics. Which parts of this song talk about hearing from God? What part of the song seems important for you to remember? Write out your answers below.

Activity #5 Obedience that pleases God or blind obedience?

Think about the game Simon Says (God Says). What is the difference between the type of obedience Christians are supposed to have (obeying what God says is true and right) and "blind obedience" (doing whatever you are told)? Write out examples of both types of obedience below.

Activity #6 Play "Mother, May I?".

Play the game Mother, May I? in order to practice following directions.

Activity #7 Is God like the "Mother" in Mother, May I?

Think about the game Mother, May I? How is this "Mother" similar to God, and how is this "Mother" NOT similar to God? Write your answer below.

Activity #8 Take the Good Shepherd Obstacle Course.

This game helps you practice carefully listening and following directions.

ART PROJECT

Project #1 "Stubborn as a Mule"
Psalm 32:8-9 says, "I will guide you and teach you the way you should go. I will give you good advice and watch over you with love. Don't be like a horse or a mule. They can't understand anything. They have to be controlled by bit and bridles. If they aren't, they won't come to you." Draw an illustration for this Bible passage.

LESSON 4

NOAH HEARD AND OBEYED

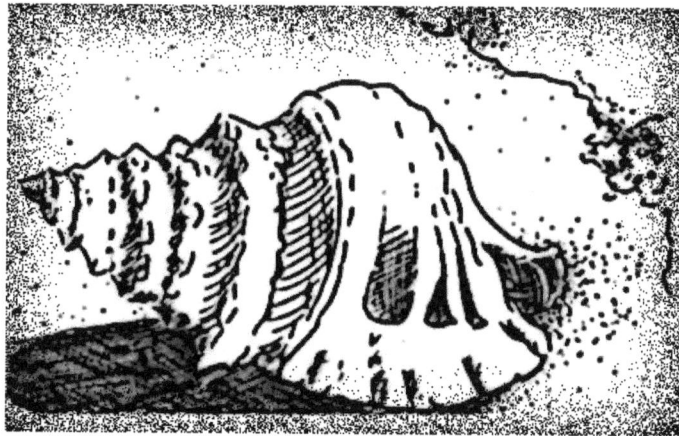

OBJECTIVE

Noah was a righteous man who heard God speaking to him. He did not stop obeying God because of what others said, and Noah didn't depend only on his own limited thinking. Noah knew God, and he trusted God to help him do what seemed impossible—to build an ark. Because he obeyed God's voice, God was able to save him, his family and the animals.

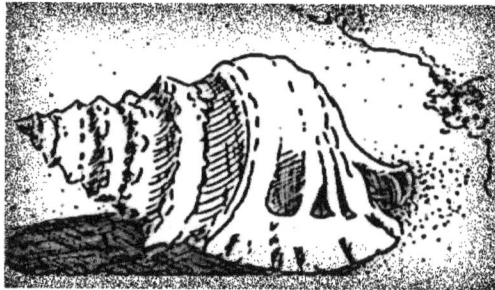

NOAH HEARD AND OBEYED

KEY SCRIPTURE

Genesis 6:22 "Noah did everything just as God commanded him."

Copy the Key Scripture for this lesson in the space below.

READING THE BOOK

Read Chapters 6 and 7 in *Is That Really You, God?*

What in this chapter seemed interesting or important to you? Write out your thoughts.

MY NOTES ON THE TEACHING

PRAYER AND MINISTRY TIME

When you think you have heard something from God that will encourage the person who will be prayed for this lesson, write what you heard below.

For instance, God may give you a verse from the Bible that will encourage that person. Or if God gives you a picture in your mind as you think about that person, ask God what the picture means. Then write what He says, or draw a picture of what you saw. Or God may give you a dream at night. If so, ask Him what it means for that person, and write it below. Share with that person what God gave you, and pray a prayer for him that is in line with what God gave you.

The person I am praying for this lesson is _____.

This is what God gave me for this person:

This is what I prayed:

Answer to prayer and date:

LEARNING ACTIVITIES

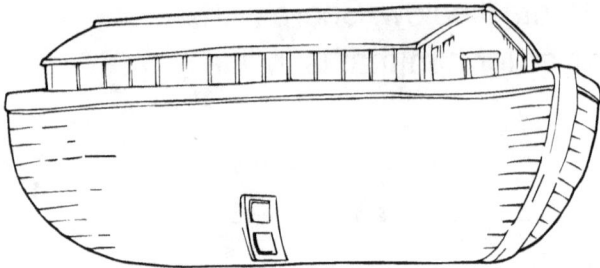

Activity #1 Make a model of the ark.

Make a model of the ark following God's instructions in Genesis 6:15-16. The scale is 450 feet = 4.5 feet long (54 inches), 75 feet = .75 feet wide (9 inches), and 45 feet = .45 feet high (5 ½ inches). Take a photograph of your finished project and attach it below.

Activity #2 Visit the Ark Encounter website.
Go to arkencounter.com. Explore this website and read explanations about the flood, the ark and Noah's family. Which pages of this website were most interesting to you?

Activity #3 Play the Freeze Game.
With this game, you can learn to obey right away and completely. It is best to play it outside or in a large room. The leader will give directions to the players. These directions will be crazy commands like walk backward while holding your nose, or crab crawl on hands and feet. Then, when the leader wants the players to stop moving, he will say, "Freeze." Any player who moves after the leader says "Freeze" is out and must sit down. The last one playing is the most obedient and wins.

Activity #4 Which animals are "clean" and "unclean"?
In **Genesis 7:2** God told Noah to bring on the ark seven pairs of every "clean" animal and only one pair of every animal that was "unclean." Go to the website gotquestions.org to find out which animals were clean and unclean. Type in: "What made some animals clean and others unclean?" List several clean and then several unclean animals.

Activity #5 Play the Coloring by Command Game.

Use the Lesson 4 Noah's Ark coloring page in your Workbook. To play the Coloring by Command Game, you should follow all coloring commands given by the leader. The more colors in your picture that match the colors that the leader calls out, the better your chance of winning. After you play the game, answer these questions:

How well were you able to match the colors the leader called out? How did it feel being told how to color the picture?

Activity #6 Committing your whole life to God
2 Chronicles 16:9a says, **"The Lord looks out over the whole earth. He gives strength to those who commit their lives completely to him."**
Write in your Workbook about what you think it would look like to commit your whole life to God.

ART PROJECTS

Project #1 Noah and the Ark Coloring Page
Turn to the next page and color in the picture.

Project #2 Make a Noah's Ark mobile.
Make a mobile of the ark and the animals from the Lesson 4 patterns in your Workbook. Trace and cut out the ark and animal patterns. Color them and staple a string to each one. Tie each string to a hanger or dowels. Make the strings different lengths. Attach a string to the hanger or dowels, using it to hang the mobile from the ceiling or wall hook. Take a photo of it and attach it here.

Project #3 Create a Noah's Ark mural.

As a family or class, make a large mural of Noah and the ark. Take a photograph of it and attach it below.

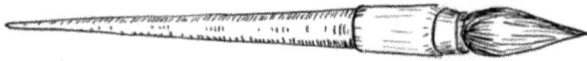

Project #4 Paint a picture of the ark.

Make a watercolor picture of the ark, animals and Noah's family. Once your painting has dried, attach it to the next page.

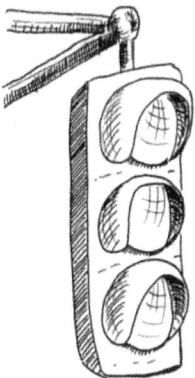

Project #5 Make a traffic light.

Think about the idea that we obey God for our own safety, just as we have to obey traffic lights and road signs for our safety.

a. Easy version - Using the Lesson 4 circle pattern at the end of your Workbook, trace and cut out one red and one green circle (the same size) out of construction paper and glue them on opposite sides of a Popsicle stick.

b. More difficult version - Cut a piece of white construction paper in half longwise (so that you have 2 tall and skinny pieces). Glue these together with the paint stirring stick between them. Leave some stick exposed at the bottom so you can hold it up. Using the Lesson 4 circle pattern at the end of your Workbook, trace three 3-inch circles on each side, in a line up and down. Use a crayon to color the red and yellow circles on one side, and the green and yellow circles on the other side. The correct order of the colors is red at the top, yellow in the middle, and green at the bottom. Using the circle pattern, trace and cut out one red circle from construction paper for one side and one green circle for the other side. Glue them on, so that these will seem brighter and easier to see than the other "lights" on the traffic light.

If you would like, you could attach a photograph of your traffic light below.

LESSON 5

SPIRIT, SOUL, BODY— OUR DIFFERENT PARTS

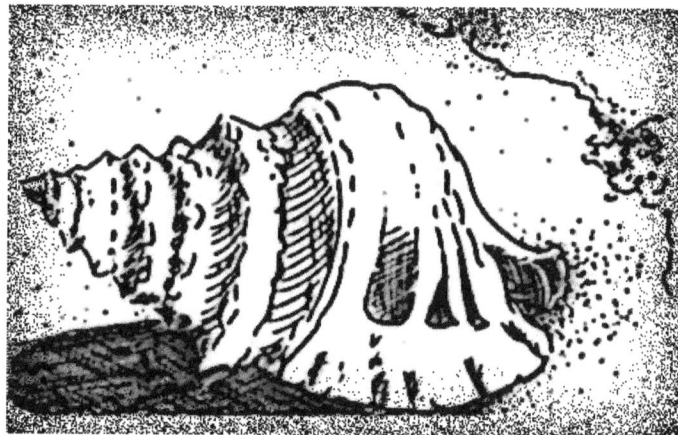

OBJECTIVE

We hear God's voice in our spirit. So, we need to understand the difference between our spirit, soul and body.

SPIRIT, SOUL, BODY—OUR DIFFERENT PARTS

KEY SCRIPTURE

1 Thessalonians 5:23 "…May he make you holy through and through. May your whole spirit, soul and body be kept free from blame…."

Copy the Key Scripture for this lesson in the space below.

READING THE BOOK

Read Chapter 8 in *Is That Really You, God?*
What in this chapter seemed interesting or important to you? Write out your thoughts.

MY NOTES ON THE TEACHING

PRAYER AND MINISTRY TIME

When you think you have heard something from God that will encourage the person who will be prayed for this lesson, write what you heard below.

For instance, God may give you a verse from the Bible that will encourage that person. Or if God gives you a picture in your mind as you think about that person, ask God what the picture means. Then write what He says, or draw a picture of what you saw. Or God may give you a dream at night. If so, ask Him what it means for that person, and write it below.

Share with that person what God gave you, and pray a prayer for him that is in line with what God gave you.

The person I am praying for this lesson is _____.

This is what God gave me for this person:

This is what I prayed:

Answer to prayer and date:

LEARNING ACTIVITIES

Activity #1 The chocolate milk illustration
After seeing the chocolate milk illustration of the spirit, soul and body, write below answers to these questions:

What does the glass represent?

What does the milk represent?

What does the chocolate syrup represent?

What can we do to make sure the Holy Spirit flavors our thinking, feelings and what we decide to do?

Activity #2 A matching challenge

Draw lines from each word on the left to what describes it on the right.
Hint: There will be more than one match for each part of you.

Body

Your mind, will and emotions

Where God speaks to you

Spirit

The physical house you live in

Tells you what to think and feel

Soul

Where God's life lives in you

Helps you see, smell, touch, taste and hear

ART PROJECTS

Project #1 Make a play-dough spirit, soul and body
Using a cookie cutter, make a play-dough gingerbread man. Shape a soul and spirit from different colored play-dough that look like the Lesson 5 patterns for the soul and spirit in the back of the Workbook. Write what you learned about the spirit, soul and body.

Project #2 Sidewalk chalk spirit, soul and body

Lay down on a driveway or sidewalk. Have someone trace around your body with sidewalk chalk. Then, get up and draw in where the soul and spirit are with different colors of chalk.

Label each part: spirit, soul and body.

What does your body help you do?

What is the soul made up of?

What is special about your spirit?

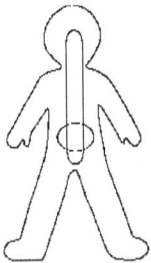

Project #3 The spirit, soul and body on paper

Make a paper person showing the spirit, soul and body. Trace the Lesson 5 patterns of the spirit, soul and body onto paper and cut out these shapes. Glue the soul and spirit on the body and label each part. Attach it below.

LESSON 6

SPIRIT, SOUL, BODY— WHO RULES?

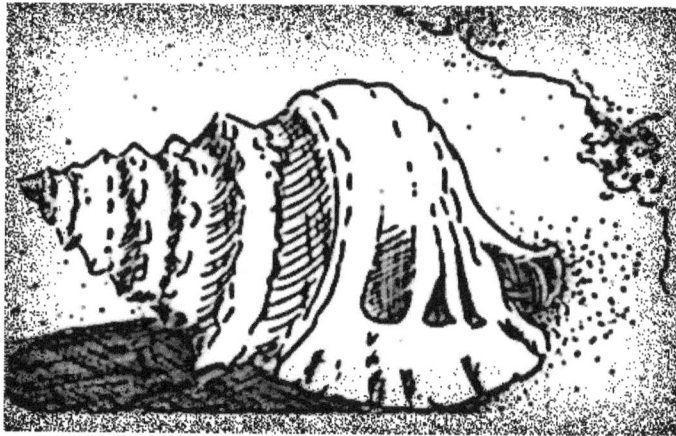

OBJECTIVE

Because we hear God's voice in our spirit,
we need to allow our spirit to rule us.

SPIRIT, SOUL AND BODY—WHO RULES?

KEY SCRIPTURE

Matthew 11:28-30 "Come to me, all you who are tired and are carrying heavy loads. I will give you rest. Become my servants and learn from me...Serving me is easy, and my load is light."

Copy the Key Scripture for this lesson in the space below.

READING THE BOOK

Read Chapter 9 in *Is That Really You, God?*
What in this chapter seemed interesting or
important to you? Write out your thoughts.

MY NOTES ON THE TEACHING

PRAYER AND MINISTRY TIME

When you think you have heard something from God that will encourage the person who will be prayed for this lesson, write what you heard below.

For instance, God may give you a verse from the Bible that will encourage that person. Or if God gives you a picture in your mind as you think about that person, ask God what the picture means. Then write what He says, or draw a picture of what you saw. Or God may give you a dream at night. If so, ask Him what it means for that person, and write it below. Share with that person what God gave you, and pray a prayer for him that is in line with what God gave you.

The person I am praying for this lesson is _____

This is what God gave me for this person:

This is what I prayed:

Answer to prayer and date:

LEARNING ACTIVITIES

Activity #1 Draw a life-size spirit, soul and body.

Lay down on a large piece of paper. Have someone trace around your entire body. Then, draw in your face, hair, fingers and toes, and so on. Draw where the spirit and soul would be on the picture of your body. Take a photograph of your picture and place it here.

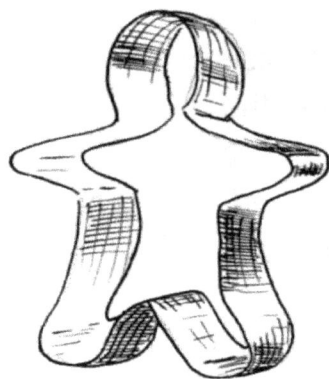

Activity #2 Make a spirit, soul and body gingerbread cookie.

Make a real gingerbread man out of cookie dough. Bake it in the oven and then let the gingerbread man cool. Using a container of icing with a nozzle, draw the outline of the soul on the cookie. Include the head, the chest and the stomach (the mind, will and emotions). With icing, glue a red candy or chocolate chip on the gingerbread man's upper abdomen where the spirit is.

While the gingerbread man is baking, write below what it is like to be ruled by the soul and what it is like to be ruled by the spirit.

When I am ruled by my soul (my own mind, will and emotions), I...

When I am ruled by my spirit, I...

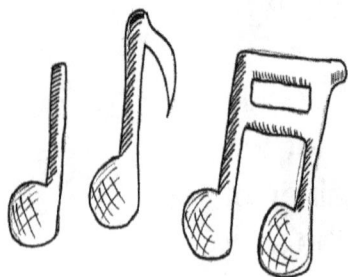

Activity #3 Why so downcast, oh my soul?
Search YouTube for the song "Acapella Praise – Why so downcast, oh my soul." Listen to the song and see how we can use praise music when we are stuck in feelings of worry or sadness. Praising God reminds us that He is good and powerful, and He loves us.

Write below the name of a praise song that helps you stop feeling worried or sad. Write out what that song says about God?

Activity #4 Let your spirit rule you.
Remember the suggestions in this lesson to let our spirit rule us:

•	If your MIND wants you to think hurtful thoughts, spend time READING THE BIBLE, GOD'S WORD.

•	If your WILL wants you to do something you shouldn't, spend time PRAYING—talking and listening to God.

•	If your EMOTIONS are stuck in a hurtful feeling like jealousy, anger or feeling sorry for yourself, spend time PRAISING GOD.

Keep your eyes open for a time this week when you need to let your spirit rule you, not your soul. Use God's Word, prayer to God or praising God to rule your mind, will and emotions. Write about a situation where you used one of the suggestions above.

ART PROJECTS

Project #1 Draw Jesus in the Garden of Gethsemane.
Read **Matthew 26:36-46** again. Draw a picture below of Jesus praying in the Garden of Gethsemane.

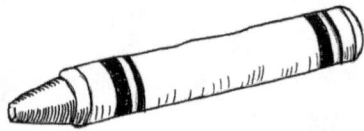

Project #2 The Disciples find Jesus Praying coloring page
MATERIALS NEEDED: Markers, crayons or colored pencils

Color in the coloring page The Disciples Find Jesus Praying, which can be found on the next page.

Project #3 Draw Jesus lightening your load.
Read **Matthew 11:28–30** again. Draw a picture of what it might look like to have Jesus give you rest by giving you a light load to carry instead of a heavy load.

LESSON 6

LESSON 7

GOD WILL HELP US

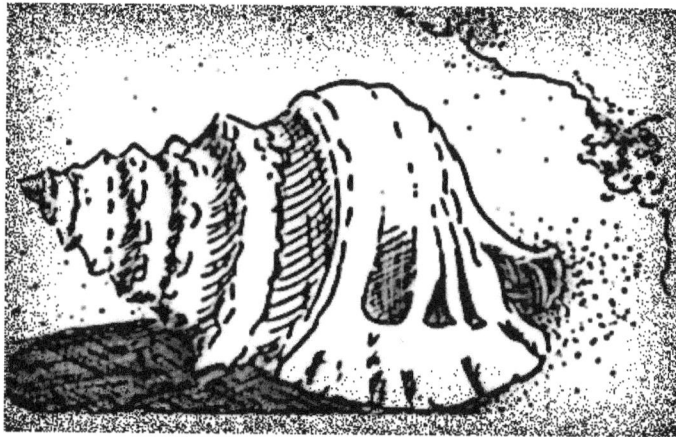

OBJECTIVE

*We should ask God for help when we feel weak,
afraid or are in trouble.*

GOD WILL HELP US

KEY SCRIPTURES

2 Chronicles 20:4 "The people came together to ask the LORD for help. In fact, they came from every town in Judah to pray to him."

Jeremiah 33:3 "Call out to me. I will answer you. I will tell you great things you do not know…."

Copy the Key Scriptures for this lesson in the space below.

READING THE BOOK

Read Chapter 10 in *Is That Really You, God?*
What in this chapter seemed interesting or important to you? Write out your thoughts.

MY NOTES ON THE TEACHING

PRAYER AND MINISTRY TIME

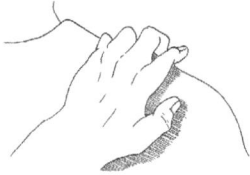

When you think you have heard something from God that will encourage the person who will be prayed for this lesson, write what you heard below.

For instance, God may give you a verse from the Bible that will encourage that person. Or if God gives you a picture in your mind as you think about that person, ask God what the picture means. Then write what He says, or draw a picture of what you saw. Or God may give you a dream at night. If so, ask Him what it means for that person, and write it below. Share with that person what God gave you, and pray a prayer for him that is in line with what God gave you.

The person I am praying for this lesson is_____.

This is what God gave me for this person:

This is what I prayed:

Answer to prayer and date:

LEARNING ACTIVITIES

Activity #1 The Holy Spirit helps us.
In Old Testament times, God placed the Holy Spirit on a few special people like kings, prophets, priests or judges. To hear from God, average people had to wait until He spoke through a prophet. But after Jesus died on the cross, rose from the dead and returned to heaven, God sent the Holy Spirit to live in anyone who believes in Jesus! Although God can still speak through a prophet, we average people can hear directly from God through His Holy Spirit.

Read **John 14:16-17; John 14:26 and John 16:13-14**, and then list what the Holy Spirit wants to do for you.

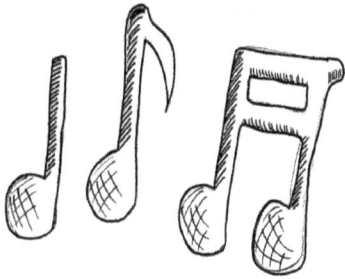

Activity #2 Praise God for what He has done for you.

List in your Workbook some of the things that God has done for you. Gather any musical instruments you have. Play the instruments while you sing along with a praise song. Worship God in your heart, telling Him how much you love Him.

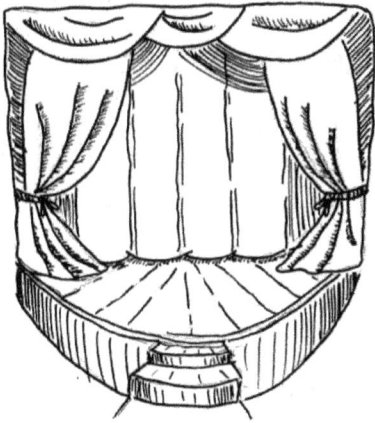

Activity #3 Act out King Jehoshaphat's battle.

Act out the story of King Jehoshaphat's defeat of Ammon, Moab and Mount Seir in **2 Chronicles 20** using props or costumes. Search YouTube for a praise song that speaks of God's goodness and power. As you march into battle, sing or play musical instruments along with this song. Write the name of the song you used to praise God below. Take a picture of the cast in your play with their props or costumes and attach it.

Activity #4 Watch videos about 2 Chronicles 20.
Search YouTube for these videos and watch them:
• Sunday School Lesson for Kids - Give Thanks to the Lord - **2 Chronicles 20** Sharefaithkids
• Awaken Dance / Jehoshaphat

ART PROJECTS

Project #1 Make a drum.
Tape the top of an oatmeal container onto the container. Glue on decorative wrapping paper. Tap the top of the drum with your fingers or a wooden spoon.

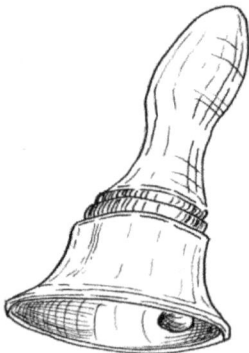

Project #2 Make a jingler.
Tie bells onto pieces of yarn. Thread the yarn through holes in the bottom of a cup, knot the yarn, and secure with tape. With the cup upside down, the jingle bells should hang inside of the cup. Shake the cup, holding the narrow end.

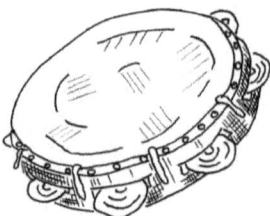

Project #3 Make a tambourine.
Cut colorful fabric streamers and tape them into one pie pan, so that they hang down from it. Place jingle bells inside of one pan, and tape the two pie pans together. Hold the tambourine with the streamers hanging down. Gently, but sharply, hit the flat side with your hand, making the bells jingle inside.

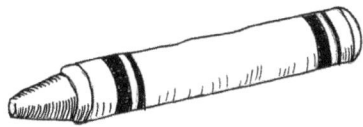

Project #4 Draw a picture from 2 Chronicles 20.

Draw a picture of one of the scenes from **2 Chronicles 20:1-28.** This could be:

- When Jehoshaphat, the men, women and children of Judah fasted and prayed to the Lord for help, and then Jahaziel heard from God.

- When the people of Judah marched out to meet the enemy, just singing and praising God.

- When they looked out over the battle field and saw that their enemies were already dead.

Project #5 Jehoshaphat and the People of Judah Praying coloring page

Turn to the next page and color in the picture. Color in the picture that shows Jehoshaphat and the people of Judah praying.

"Jehoshaphat bowed down with his face toward the ground. All the people of Judah and Jerusalem also bowed down. They worshiped the Lord."

"Jehoshaphat... appointed men to sing to the Lord. He wanted them to praise the Lord because of his glory and holiness."

"As they began to sing and praise, the Lord set ambushes against the men of Ammon and Moab and Mount Seir who were invading Judah, and they were defeated."

2 Chronicles 20:18, 21-22

LESSON 8

OBEYING GOD IS BEST

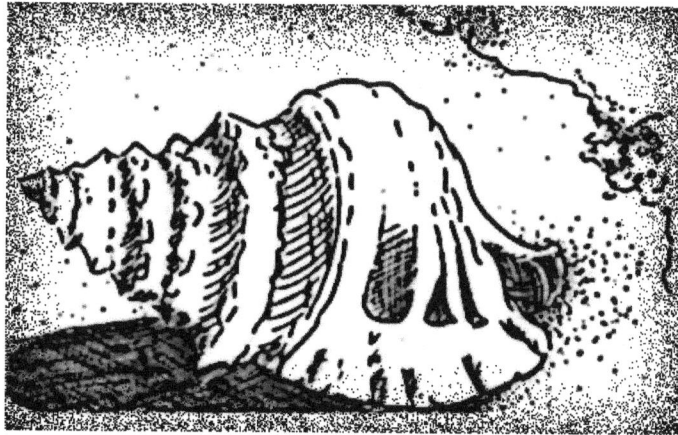

OBJECTIVE

There are obstacles that get in the way of our hearing and obeying God's voice. When we remove them, we will be able to listen and obey. Obeying God is always best for us.

OBEYING GOD IS BEST

KEY SCRIPTURES

1 Samuel 15:22 "What pleases the Lord more?…It is better to obey than to offer a sacrifice."

1 John 1:9 "…If we admit that we have sinned, he will forgive us our sins. He will forgive every wrong thing we have done. He will make us pure."

Copy the Key Scriptures for this lesson in the space below.

READING THE BOOK

Read Chapters 11 and 12 in *Is That Really You, God?*
What in these chapters seemed interesting or important to you? Write out your thoughts.

MY NOTES ON THE TEACHING

PRAYER AND MINISTRY TIME

When you think you have heard something from God that will encourage the person who will be prayed for this lesson, write what you heard below.

For instance, God may give you a verse from the Bible that will encourage that person. Or if God gives you a picture in your mind as you think about that person, ask God what the picture means. Then write what He says, or draw a picture of what you saw. Or God may give you a dream at night. If so, ask Him what it means for that person, and write it below. Share with that person what God gave you, and pray a prayer for him that is in line with what God gave you.

The person I am praying for this lesson is _____.

This is what God gave me for this person:

This is what I prayed:

Answer to prayer and date:

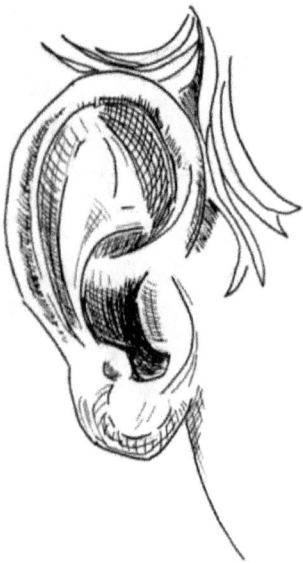

LEARNING ACTIVITIES

Activity #1 What keeps you from hearing and obeying God?
Look at the list of things below that keep us from hearing God clearly. Circle the things that are a problem in your life.

a. We don't know how to hear God.

b. We don't spend time with God by reading the Bible, talking to Him or worshiping.

c. We have not confessed sins to God and received His forgiveness.

d. We have not forgiven someone.

e. We don't believe God is able to speak to us or help us.

f. We are afraid of what might happen if we obey God.

g. We are afraid of what people might think about us if we obey God.

Write a prayer to God, asking for His forgiveness and help in those areas.

Activity #2 Which king is it?

Write on the lines below the names of the kings that match the lists underneath. Which list describes King Saul? Which list describes King Jehoshaphat?

_____	_____
Knew God well	Didn't know God well
Depended on God's help	Depended on himself and others
Wanted to please God	Wanted to please others
When wrong, was truly sorry	When wrong, made excuses or lied
Knew and loved the Word	Didn't know or love what God said in scripture or through his prophet
Never turned away from God	Turned away from God

Activity #3 Watch a video about God rejecting Saul as king.
Search YouTube for a video titled "Samuel Rebukes King Saul – Superbook" and watch it together. Share what you thought of this video.

Activity #4 Jesus washes us whiter than snow.
Together, bake chocolate cupcakes and frost them with white frosting. The dark cupcake represents our sin and the white frosting represents us when we have been cleansed whiter than snow by Jesus. If you choose to, you could use chocolate graham crackers instead of baking cupcakes.

Another snack idea would be cream cheese spread on dark bread.

Activity #5 Play Chutes and Ladders.
Together, play the board game Chutes and Ladders, to see how one move can make you go in a completely different direction.

Can you think of a decision that you made that changed the direction in your life? Write about that below.

Activity #6 Watch a video about making choices and obeying God.
Search YouTube for the video "Do the Bright Thing" 1/3 and 2/3 from the McGee and Me series by Focus on the Family.

Write below the answers to these questions: Did the main character seem more like King Jehoshaphat or King Saul? Why do you think that?

ART PROJECT

Project #1 Jesus is King.

Create a crown to wear. Using the Lesson 8 crown pattern found at the back of your Workbook, trace sections of a crown on gold-colored paper. Cut out enough crown sections so that stapled or taped together, they will fit on your head. Before attaching the ends, write "Jesus is King" on the crown and decorate it. When you are finished, attach the ends of the crown together so it will fit on your head.

Jesus is King of our lives when we listen to the Holy Spirit in our spirit. We make ourselves king, instead of Jesus, when we listen to our soul and do something that God would not want us to do. Who will rule in your life?

If you would like, staple your crown below.

LESSON 9

HEARING GOD THROUGH THE INNER KNOWING

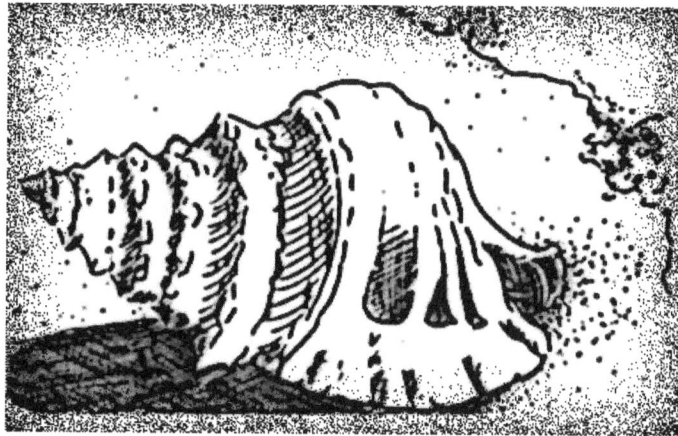

OBJECTIVE

God often communicates through an inner knowing. When God speaks to us through an inner knowing, He does not use words. Instead, He gives us either a "knowing that you know," a sense of peace, a sudden lack of peace, or the idea to slow down and wait.

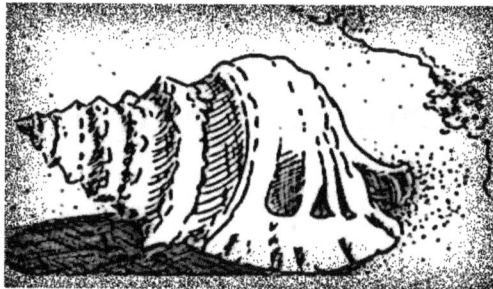

HEARING GOD THROUGH THE INNER KNOWING

KEY SCRIPTURE

Isaiah 41:13 "I am the LORD your God. I take hold of your right hand. I say to you, 'Do not be afraid. I will help you.'"

Copy the Key Scripture for this lesson in the space below.

READING THE BOOK

Read Chapters 13 and 14 in *Is That Really You, God?*
What in these chapters seemed interesting or important to you? Write out your thoughts.

MY NOTES ON THE TEACHING

PRAYER AND MINISTRY TIME

When you think you have heard something from God that will encourage the person who will be prayed for this lesson, write what you heard below.

For instance, God may give you a verse from the Bible that will encourage that person. Or if God gives you a picture in your mind as you think about that person, ask God what the picture means. Then write what He says, or draw a picture of what you saw. Or God may give you a dream at night. If so, ask Him what it means for that person, and write it below. Share with that person what God gave you, and pray a prayer for him that is in line with what God gave you.

The person I am praying for this lesson is _____.

This is what God gave me for this person:

This is what I prayed:

Answer to prayer and date:

LEARNING ACTIVITIES

Activity #1 Play the game Follow Your Guide. To play, one player will wear a blindfold. Another person will guide him across a room that has obstacles in the way. The goal is to get the blindfolded person across the room without falling or hitting something—all without using words. When it is your turn to be blindfolded, hold the hand of your guide. Let him guide you around objects, paying attention to the silent signals he gives you.

When it is your turn to be the guide, take the blindfolded player's hand and silently walk across the room together. Stop when you come to an object in the way. Then guide the person around that object without saying a word, and continue on across the room.

Did you understand what your guide was trying to say to you even though he didn't use words? Write about what it was like to be blindfolded and led.

Activity #2 Play Red Light/Green Light.

To play, one person plays the role of "traffic light" and the rest try to touch him. To start, all the children form a line more than 30 feet away from the traffic light.

The traffic light faces away from you and calls "Green light." Then you are allowed to move towards the traffic light, to try to touch him.

At any point, the traffic light may call "Red light!" and then turn around. You who are caught moving after he turns around are "out" and must sit down. Play starts again when the traffic light turns back around and calls "Green light."

The traffic light wins if all the children are out before anyone is able to touch him. Otherwise, the first player to touch the traffic light wins the game and earns the right to be the traffic light for the next game.

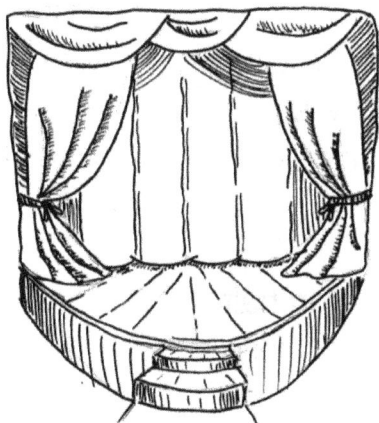

Activity #3 Act out the scriptures with a resistance band.

First, use the stretchy band to be like the Holy Spirit in **Acts 16:6-10**. In these verses the Holy Spirit kept Paul from going into Asia Minor and Bithynia. Obviously, the Holy Spirit does not use stretchy bands! Write below how the Holy Spirit may have told Paul not to go there.

Then, use the stretchy band to be like the Holy Spirit in **Acts 20:22-24.** In these verses, the Holy Spirit compelled Paul to want to go to Jerusalem. Again, the Holy Spirit does not use stretchy bands! Write below how Paul might have known that the Holy Spirit wanted him to go to Jerusalem.

ART PROJECTS

Project #1 Make a traffic light.

If you did not create a traffic light in Lesson 4, do that now. Then think about situations in which God could speak through a "traffic light" in your heart.

a. Easy version - Using the Lesson 4 circle pattern at the end of your Workbook, trace and cut out one red and one green circle (the same size) out of construction paper and glue them on opposite sides of a Popsicle stick.

b. More difficult version - Cut a piece of white construction paper in half lengthwise (so that you have 2 tall and skinny pieces.) Glue these together with the paint-stirring stick between them. Leave some stick exposed at the bottom so you can hold it up. Using the Lesson 4 circle pattern at the end of your Workbook, trace three same-sized circles on each side in a line up and down. Use a crayon to color the red and yellow circles on one side, and the green and yellow circles on the other side. The correct order of the colors is red at the top, yellow in the middle, and green at the bottom. Using the circle pattern, trace and cut out one red circle from construction paper for one side and one green circle for the other side, and glue them on. These will seem brighter and easier to see than the other "lights" on the traffic light.

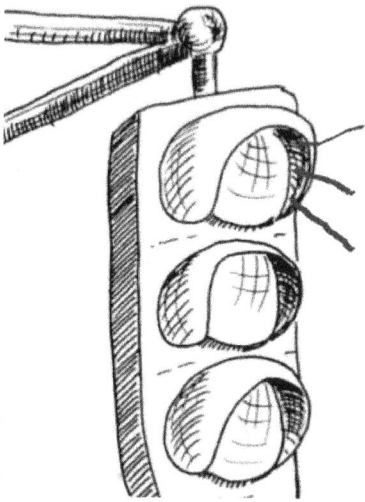

Below, write about a situation in which God could speak to you using a "red light."

Write about a situation in which God could speak to you using a "green light."

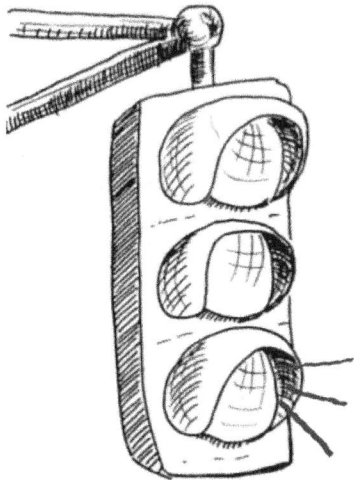

Write about a situation in which God could speak to you using a "yellow light."

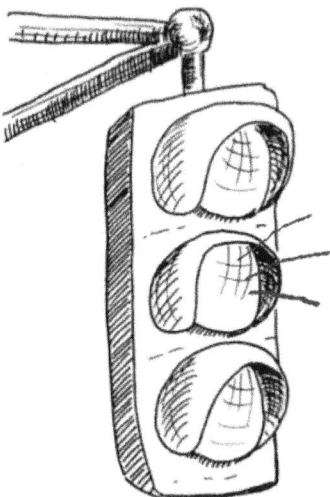

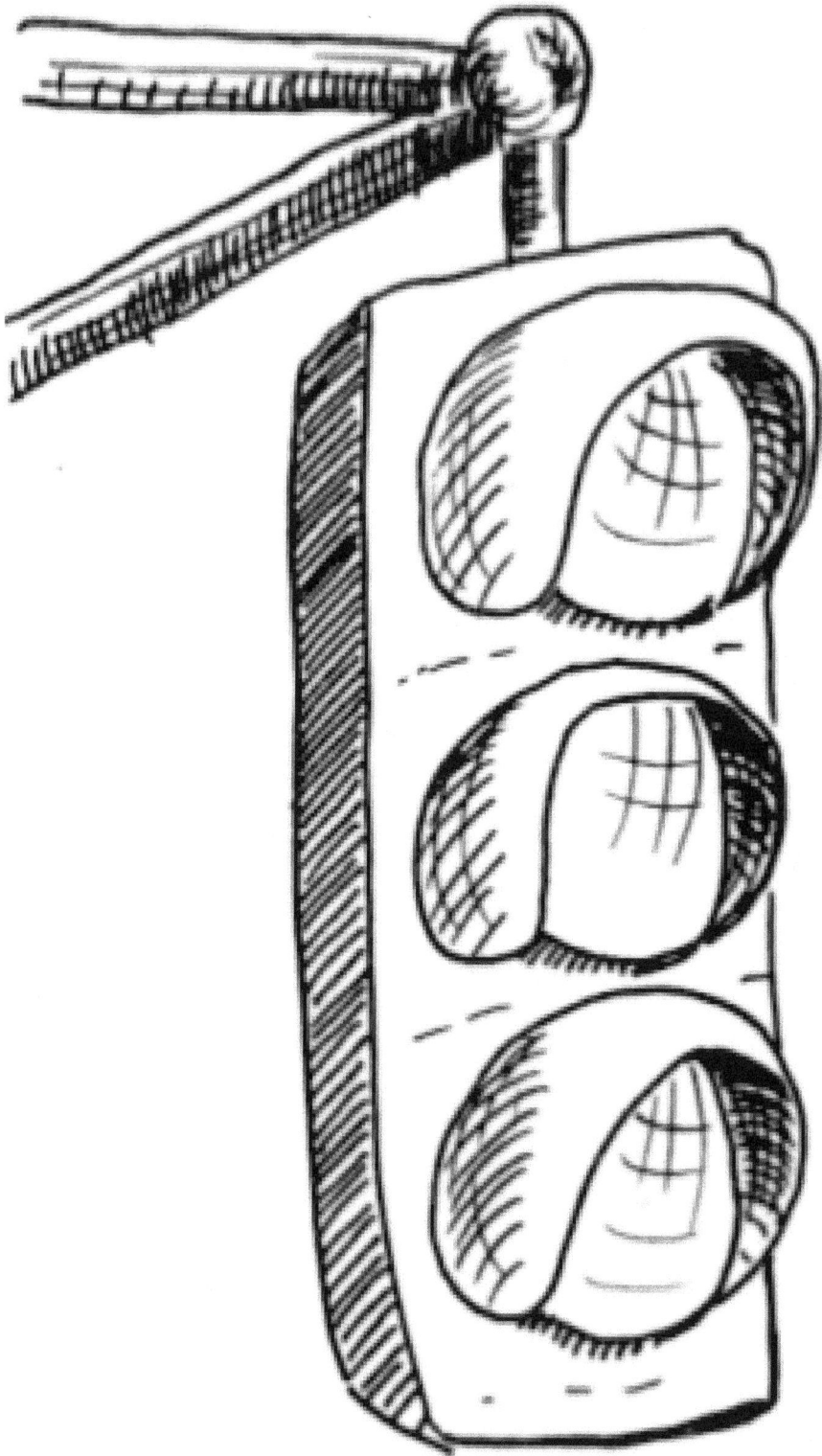

Red = Stop!

Yellow = Wait on God

Green = Go Ahead

LESSON 10

HEARING GOD THROUGH THE SOFT, INNER VOICE

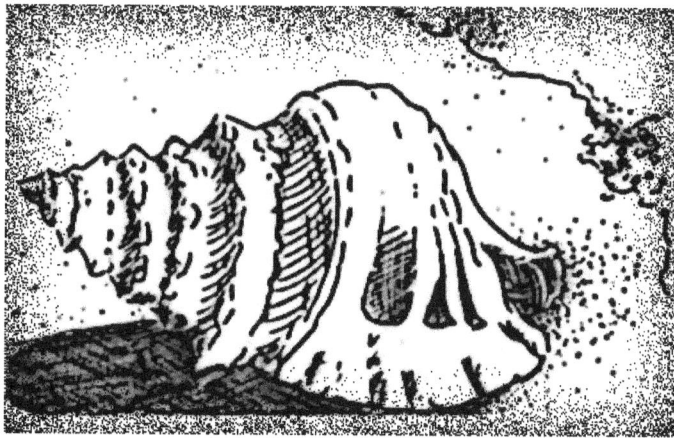

OBJECTIVE

Sometimes God speaks to us through the inner voice. This is when the Holy Spirit speaks in a quiet voice using words. We need to listen carefully to hear God's soft voice.

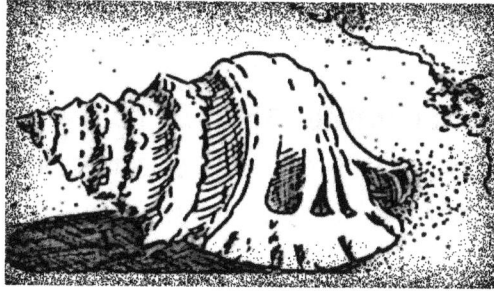

HEARING GOD THROUGH THE SOFT, INNER VOICE

KEY SCRIPTURE

Isaiah 30:21 "You will hear your Teacher's voice behind you. You will hear it whether you turn to the right or the left. It will say, 'Here is the path I want you to take. So walk on it.'"

Copy the Key Scripture for this lesson in the space below.

READING THE BOOK

Read Chapter 15 in *Is That Really You, God?* What in this chapter seemed interesting or important to you? Write out your thoughts.

MY NOTES ON THE TEACHING

PRAYER AND MINISTRY TIME

When you think you have heard something from God that will encourage the person who will be prayed for this lesson, write what you heard below.

For instance, God may give you a verse from the Bible that will encourage that person. Or if God gives you a picture in your mind as you think about that person, ask God what the picture means. Then write what He says, or draw a picture of what you saw. Or God may give you a dream at night. If so, ask Him what it means for that person, and write it below. Share with that person what God gave you, and pray a prayer for him that is in line with what God gave you.

The person I am praying for this lesson is _____.

This is what God gave me for this person:

This is what I prayed:

Answer to prayer and date:

LEARNING ACTIVITIES

Activity #1 Play the game Hot or Cold.
In this game your parent or teacher will help you find a hidden object or person by whispering directions to you. The help will come in a whisper in order to sound like the Holy Spirit speaking in your spirit with the soft, inner voice. When you are going in the wrong direction and away from the hidden object or person, you will hear the word "cold" whispered. When you are going in the right direction and towards the hidden object or person, you will hear the word "warm" whispered. And when you are very close, you will hear the word "hot." As you practice, you will get better and better at hearing and following that quiet voice.

Write below about trying to follow the directions in the soft, whispered voice. Did it take a while to figure out which direction to go? How hard was it to hear the whispered words?

Activity #2 Play the Quiet Sound Bingo game.

When you hear a sound that you have a picture for on your game board, place a marker on that sound picture. If you hear and mark EVERY sound on your game board, yell "BINGO!" and you will be the winner!

Write below about playing the Quiet Sound Bingo game. Was it easy or hard to recognize the soft sounds and match them to a picture? Did you have to wait a long time to hear a sound that matched a picture on your game board? Did you win a game?

Activity #3 Play the Scripture Hunt game.

If you played the Scripture Hunt game, look at the scriptures on clues #1 through #9.

Which scripture seems the most important to you and your life right now? Write out that scripture below and explain why it is important to you.

Activity #4 Make peanut butter and jelly sandwiches.

Just as the peanut butter and jelly work together inside the pieces of bread, the Holy Spirit and God's Word work together inside of us. Explain below how the Holy Spirit and God's Word work together inside us. For example, has the Holy Spirit ever spoken to you through a verse? If so, which verse was it and what do you think He was saying to you?

ART PROJECTS

Project #1 Create a Quiet Sound Bingo Game.

To make four game boards, cut in half two 8 ½ x 11-inch pieces of card stock. With a pencil and a ruler, draw a grid of lines, dividing each of the four game boards into six squares. In each square, glue a picture of an item that makes a quiet sound. The pictures can be found at the end of this lesson. Make enough copies of the sound-pictures to fill in the squares of four different game boards. The sound-pictures are listed in the parentheses below. From the 14 suggested sounds, select the 12 sounds you will make. Include a different mix of pictures on all four game boards. Make sure every sound that you will make is represented on at least one game board. Write your 12 sounds (found in bold) on index cards.

- **water** – slowly pour water into a glass (the drop of water)
- **eraser** – erase a pencil mark with a pencil eraser (the pencil with an eraser)
- **owl** – quietly say, "Hoo, Hoo" (the owl)
- **wind** – blow continuously through pursed lips (the cloud blowing wind)
- **ripping paper** – slowly rip a piece of paper (the rectangle with a jagged line halfway through it)
- **knock** – quietly knock on a book (the door)
- **bird** – if you can, make a bird sound by whistling (the bird)
- **dice** – roll the dice on the table (the two dice)
- **clicking pen** – click a pen open and shut (the pen that clicks)
- **scotch tape** – rip off a piece of tape from the dispenser (the scotch tape dispenser)
- **panting** – stick your tongue out and pant like a dog (the dog)
- **knuckles** – If you can, crack your knuckles (the hand)
- **pepper** – turn a pepper grinder a few times (the pepper grinder)
- **cracker** – crunch a cracker (the cracker)

Project #2 Make a Bible bookmark.

To make a Bible bookmark, cut a piece of card stock about 6 inches long and 2 inches wide. Cut a piece of ribbon, or yarn, 8 inches long. Punch a hole ¼ inch from the top and insert one end of the ribbon through it. Tie a knot in the ribbons at the top of the bookmark, so that the two loose ends can be seen when the bookmark is in a Bible. Draw a picture or design on the bookmark. Or you could write out a favorite verse on the bookmark.

Attach your bookmark or a photograph of it. Or, if you wrote a favorite verse on it, write that verse out below.

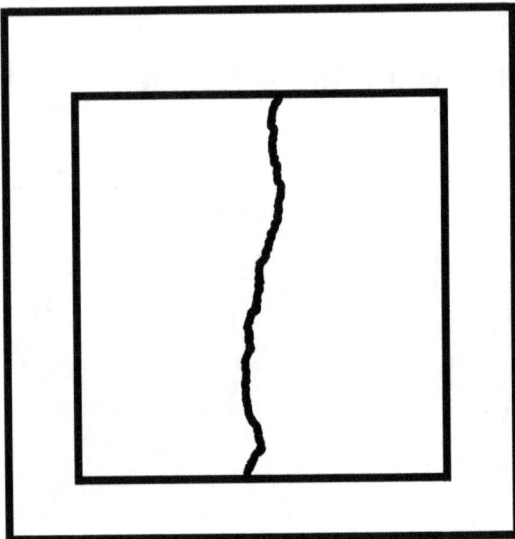

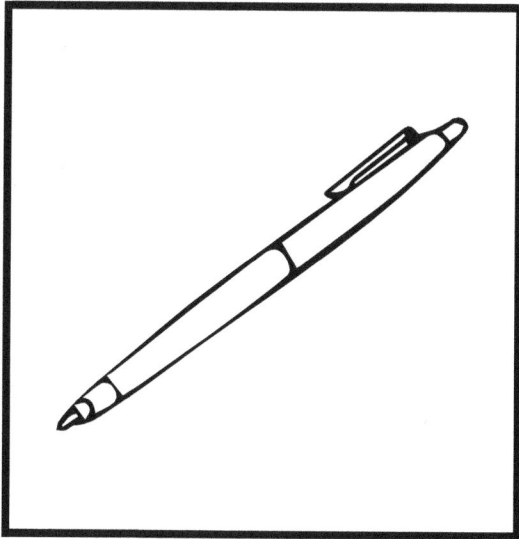
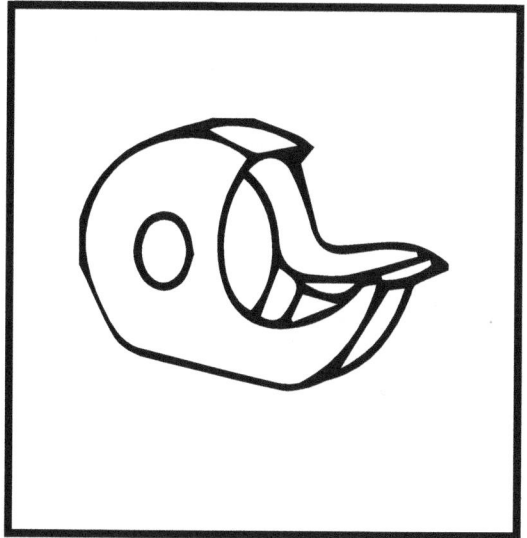

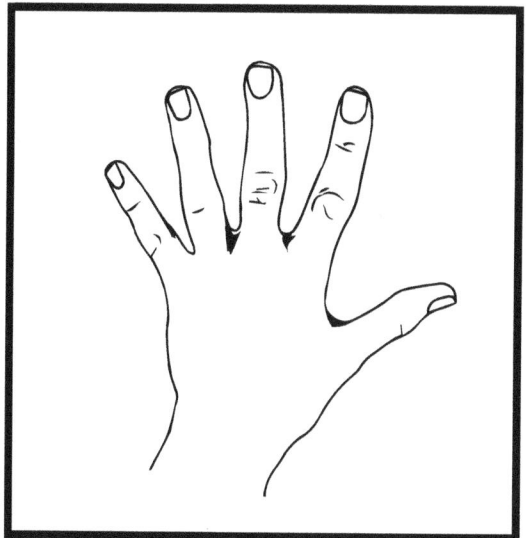

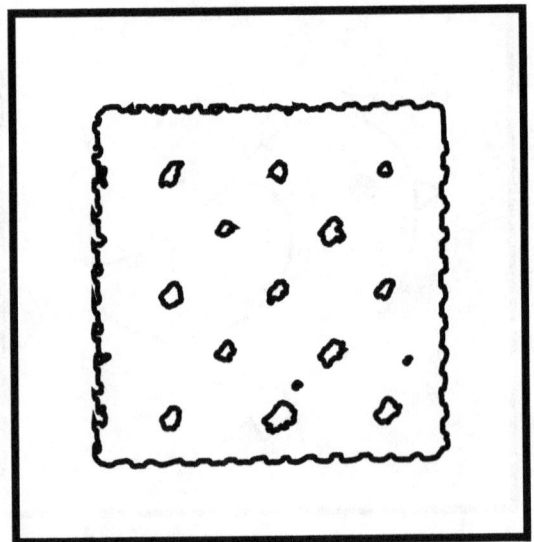

LESSON 11

HEARING GOD THROUGH THE LOUD VOICE OF THE HOLY SPIRIT

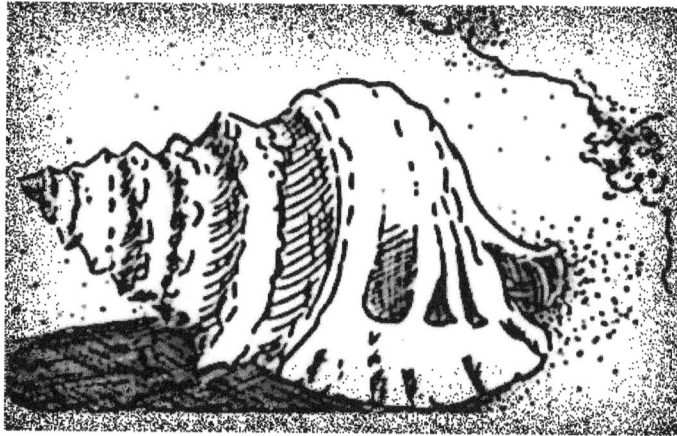

OBJECTIVE

Sometimes God speaks to us in a loud voice using words. It can also be called the authoritative voice of the Holy Spirit. It seems so loud that we think people around us can hear it too, but they can't. The Holy Spirit speaks these loud words in our spirit.

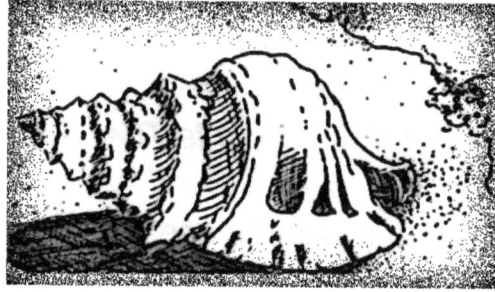

HEARING GOD THROUGH THE LOUD VOICE OF THE HOLY SPIRIT

KEY SCRIPTURE

1 Samuel 3:10 "The Lord came and called as before. He said, 'Samuel! Samuel!' And Samuel replied, 'Speak, your servant is Listening'" (NLT).

Or shorten the verse for younger children:
1 Samuel 3:10 "And Samuel replied, 'Speak, your servant is listening'" (NLT).

Copy the Key Scripture for this lesson in the space below.

READING THE BOOK

Read Chapter 16 in *Is That Really You, God?*

What in this chapter seemed interesting or important to you? Write out your thoughts.

MY NOTES ON THE TEACHING

PRAYER AND MINISTRY TIME

When you think you have heard something from God that will encourage the person who will be prayed for this lesson, write what you heard below.

For instance, God may give you a verse from the Bible that will encourage that person. Or if God gives you a picture in your mind as you think about that person, ask God what the picture means. Then write what He says, or draw a picture of what you saw. Or God may give you a dream at night. If so, ask Him what it means for that person, and write it below. Share with that person what God gave you, and pray a prayer for him that is in line with what God gave you.

The person I am praying for this lesson is _____.

This is what God gave me for this person:

This is what I prayed:

Answer to prayer and date:

LEARNING ACTIVITIES

Activity #1 Eating something black and white
Write out **Psalm 139:9-12** below.

Activity #2 Identifying familiar loud sounds
Your parent or teacher played a recording of different loud sounds. Some of the sounds were probably easy to recognize and some more difficult. List below the names of sounds that you recognized.

Activity #3 Play Follow God's Voice.
Write below the answers to these questions:
Were you able to get through the obstacle course without running into anything?

Was it difficult following the directions exactly?

Do you think you would be able to obey God if He spoke to you in His loud, authoritative voice?

Have you sensed God speaking to you more during the day or at night?
Write below about a time you sensed God speaking to you at night.

Activity #4 Listen to Songs About Hearing From God
Search YouTube for the song "Speak, O Lord – Keith and Kristyn Getty." This song begins with the same words that Samuel spoke when God called to him.

Also search YouTube for the song "Speak to Me, Lord" by Rebecca St. James. Which of these two songs is better at saying what is in your heart?

ART PROJECT

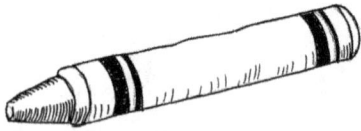

Project #1 Young Samuel hears the authoritative voice of God.

Color in the Lesson 11 Samuel coloring page on the next page with crayons. Lightly brush over your picture with watered-down black tempera paint, making it look like nighttime.

LESSON 11

LESSON 12

GOD HAS MANY DIFFERENT WAYS

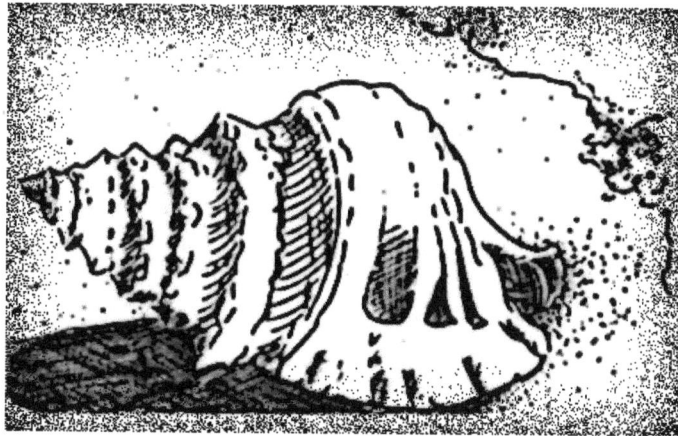

OBJECTIVE

God has many different ways of guiding us. We know that God does what is best. He may choose to guide us in a simple way or in an exciting, dramatic way. We leave it up to Him to decide how He will speak to us.

GOD HAS MANY DIFFERENT WAYS

KEY SCRIPTURE

Isaiah 55:8-9 "'My thoughts are not like your thoughts. And your ways are not like my ways,' announces the Lord. 'The heavens are higher than the earth. And my ways are higher than your ways. My thoughts are higher than your thoughts.'"

Copy the Key Scripture for this lesson in the space below.

READING THE BOOK

Read Chapters 17 and 18 in *Is That Really You, God?*
What in these chapters seemed interesting or important to you?
Write out your thoughts.

MY NOTES ON THE TEACHING

PRAYER AND MINISTRY TIME

When you think you have heard something from God that will encourage the person who will be prayed for this lesson, write what you heard below.

For instance, God may give you a verse from the Bible that will encourage that person. Or if God gives you a picture in your mind as you think about that person, ask God what the picture means. Then write what He says, or draw a picture of what you saw. Or God may give you a dream at night. If so, ask Him what it means for that person, and write it below. Share with that person what God gave you, and pray a prayer for him that is in line with what God gave you.

The person I am praying for this lesson is _____.

This is what God gave me for this person:

This is what I prayed:

Answer to prayer and date:

LEARNING ACTIVITIES

Activity #1 Worship God for His greatness and creativity in speaking to us.

Spend time praising the Lord together. In order for your worship to be heart-felt, first list all the wonderful things God has done in your life lately. List God's characteristics, what He is like. List places in nature where you see God's creativity.

Then, verbally praise the Lord for who He is and what He has done. Tell the Lord your thoughts about Him. For example, you could tell the Lord, "God, You are a great God! You are mighty! You are wonderful! I love how you gave zebras stripes! Thank You for providing everything I need. Lord, I praise You! Lord, I love You!"

Or instead, you could express your admiration for God by reading aloud a favorite psalm, or read **Psalm 150** together and praise the Lord! If you choose this option, write below which psalm you chose and which verses you like best.

Activity #2 A Rap Song

Search YouTube for a rap song that talks about hearing from God. To find an example, go to Youtube and type in "MC Jin – Over the Edge ft. Davon music video." Memorize and perform this song or another one you like. Or instead, you could write additional verses to the song and include them here.

Activity #3 Watch a video about how Paul came to believe in Jesus.

Search YouTube for a video titled "Paul's Ministry Saddleback Kids" and watch it together.

Activity #4 Visions in the Bible

Read in the Bible about other times that God used visions to speak to people. Read **Isaiah 6:1-8** and **Revelation 1:12-17**, and write what happened in these visions below.

ART PROJECTS

Project #1 God speaks to us through dreams.

Has God ever given you a dream that might be telling you something? If so, draw a picture of what God showed you.

Write what you think the Lord was saying to you through the dream.

Project #2 God speaks through visions.

Draw or paint a picture of one of the visions described in the Bible. Some Bible accounts of visions can be found in **Acts 16:9-10; Isaiah 6:1-8** and **Revelation 1:12-17.**

Project #3 Illustrate the Scriptures.

Our God is creative, and He uses many creative ways to speak to us. He has given us the ability to be creative also. Create something that represents a scene from one of the Bible passages you read in this lesson. You could use clay or play-dough to re-create a character, make a drawing of a scene in that passage, make a collage that expresses an idea in that passage from magazine pictures and words, create a diorama of that passage, etc.

Place a photograph of your creation, or create a picture below.

LESSON 13

GO AND TELL

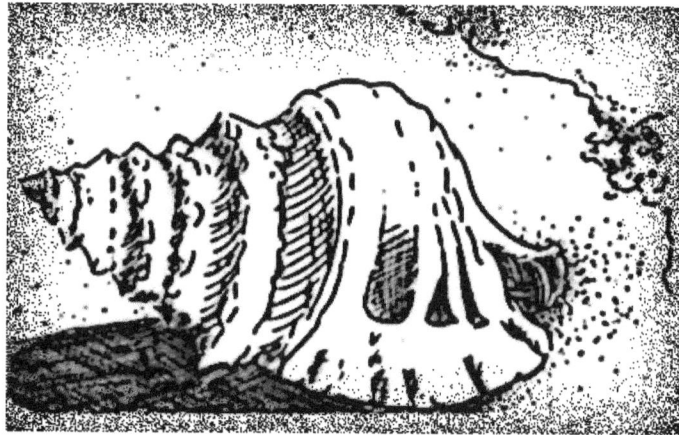

OBJECTIVE

*It is very important that we tell other people about
Jesus and what He has done for us. We want them
to hear God's voice and to have Him as their Shepherd.
We want them to have eternal life too! If we are willing to
follow what the Holy Spirit tells us to do, He will lead us to
people He has made ready to hear about Jesus. We need
to persistently pray for the people in our lives who don't
believe in Him, loving them with Jesus' love.*

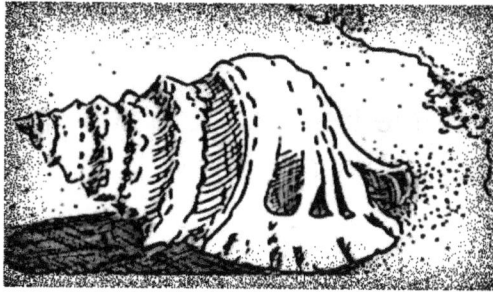

GO AND TELL

KEY SCRIPTURES

Matthew 28:19-20 "So you must go and make disciples of all nations. Baptize them in the name of the Father and of the Son and of the Holy Spirit. Teach them to obey everything I have commanded you. And you can be sure that I am always with you, to the very end."

Younger children may want to learn this shorter verse:
Mark 16:15 "He said to them, 'Go into all the world. Preach the good news to everyone.'"

Copy the Key Scripture for this lesson in the space below.

READING THE BOOK

Copy the Key Scripture you chose for this lesson in the space below.

Read Chapters 19, 20 and Twelve Points to Remember in *Is That Really You, God?*

What in these chapters seemed interesting or important to you? Write out your thoughts.

MY NOTES ON THE TEACHING

PRAYER AND MINISTRY TIME

Think of people who do not yet know about Jesus or who have not yet asked Him into their hearts. Ask God whom He wants you to pray for, to come to know Him.

People who don't know about Jesus or have not asked Him into their hearts include:

The person(s) I am praying will come to faith in Jesus is (are):

_____.

Answer to prayer and date:

LEARNING ACTIVITIES

Activity #1 Feature a missionary.
Learn about someone who is working as a missionary now. Write letters or draw pictures for the missionary, to encourage him. Or send letters and pictures for the people the missionary works with, to tell them about Jesus. Take a photo of your picture or letter and attach it below.

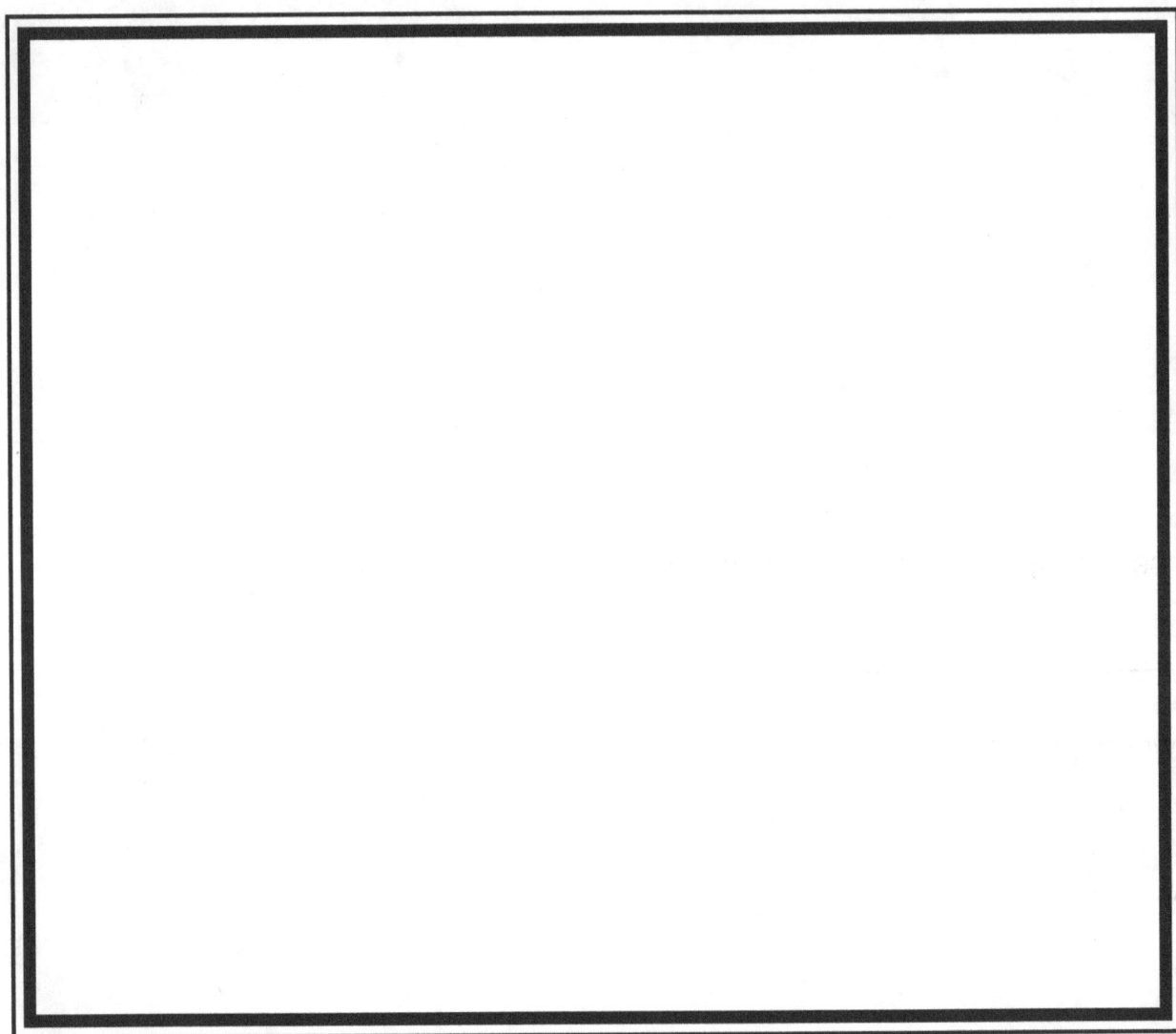

Activity #2 Be ready to share the good news.

Ask God what to say to a friend who doesn't know Jesus yet. Write below what your friend needs to know about Jesus. Practice saying what you wrote. Then be ready to share the good news with that person when God gives you the "green light."

ART PROJECT

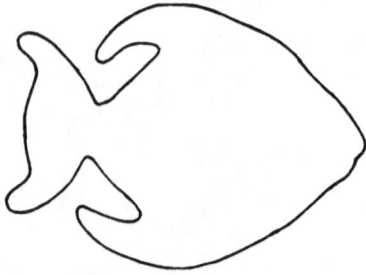

Project #1 Make a fish badge or necklace.
The fish shape reminds us that we are followers of Jesus and we get to be "fishers of people."

Cut out and trace the Lesson 13 fish pattern on colored construction paper. Print your name on it. Glue a safety pin on the back with a glue gun to make a fish-shaped badge to wear. Or you could use a hole punch and ribbon or yarn to make a fish necklace to wear. Attach your badge or necklace here when you are finished wearing it.

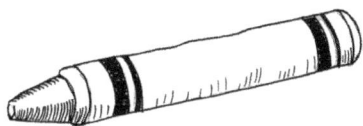

Project #2 Make a "Wordless Book."
You can make a book to help you tell others about Jesus. Draw pictures that show what you want to say about Jesus. Some picture ideas might be:

- Jesus letting children sit on His lap, to show how much He loves children.
- Jesus helping Peter pull in a net full of fish, to show He can do miracles.
- Jesus healing a lame man, to show that He wants to heal people.
- Jesus on the cross telling John to take care of His mother, Mary. This reminds us to accept Jesus' love for us so that we can love other people well.
- Mary Magdalene kneeling before Jesus at the empty tomb after He was raised from the dead. This reminds us that God rewards us when we seek Him with all our heart.
- Jesus breathing on the disciples and saying, "Receive the Holy Spirit." This reminds us that we receive the Holy Spirit when we are born again.
- Other pictures that say something about Jesus.

Three-hole punch the covers and picture pages, and hold them together with brads or yarn. Take a photo of your book and attach it here.

SALVATION
SCRIPTURES

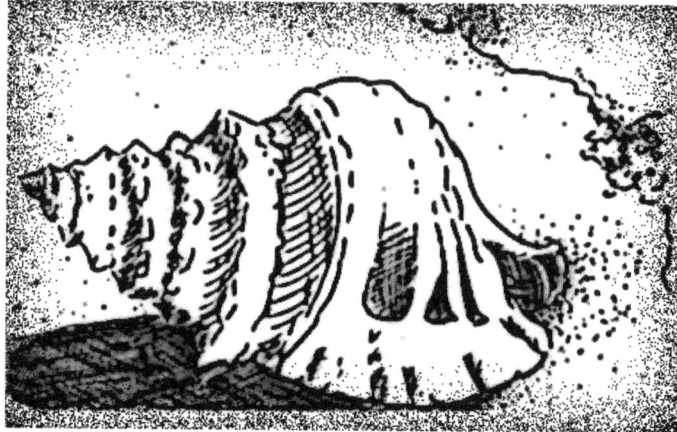

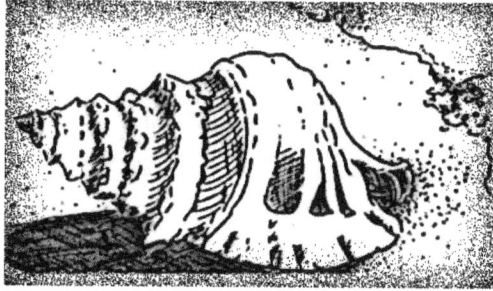

SALVATION SCRIPTURES

1. **Preparation for Salvation (being born again)**
   a. John 3:16 NIrV

   "God so loved the world that he gave his one and only Son. Anyone who believes in him will not die but will have eternal life."

   b. Romans 3:23

   "Everyone has sinned. No one measures up to God's glory."

   c. Romans 6:23

   "When you sin, the pay you get is death. But God gives you the gift of eternal life. That's because of what Christ Jesus our Lord has done."

   d. John 1:12-13

   "Some people did accept him and did believe in his name. He gave them the right to become children of God. To be a child of God has nothing to do with human parents. Children of God are not born because of human choice or because a husband wants them to be born. They are born because of what God does."

   e. John 7:37-39

   "It was the last and most important day of the feast. Jesus stood up and spoke in a loud voice. He said, 'Let anyone who is thirsty come to me and drink. Does anyone believe in me? Then, just as Scripture says, rivers of living water will flow from inside them.' When he said this, he meant the Holy Spirit. Those who believed in Jesus would receive the Spirit later. Up to that time, the Spirit had not been given. This was because Jesus had not yet received glory."

2. Confession/Prayer

Romans 10:9-11

"Say with your mouth, 'Jesus is Lord.' Believe in your heart that God raised him from the dead. Then you will be saved. With your heart you believe and are made right with God. With your mouth you say what you believe. And so you are saved. Scripture says, 'The one who believes in him will never be put to shame.'"

3. What Has Happened?

a. Romans 10:13

   "Scripture says, 'Everyone who calls on the name of the Lord will be saved.'"

b. Ezekiel 36:26-27

   "I will give you new hearts. I will give you a new spirit that is faithful to me. I will remove your stubborn hearts from you. I will give you hearts that obey me. I will put my Spirit in you. I will make you want to obey my rules. I want you to be careful to keep my laws."

4. Follow-Up

a. Read the book of John to learn more about Jesus and the new relationship you have with Him.

b. Talk with mature Christians and ask any questions you have. Go with them to church.

PATTERNS AND COLORING PAGES FOR ACTIVITIES AND PROJECTS

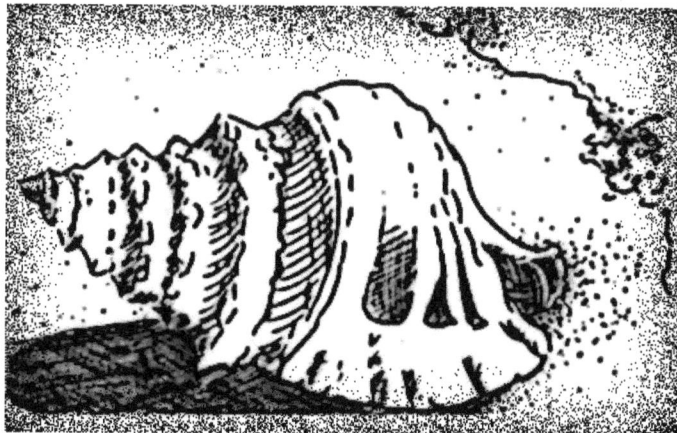

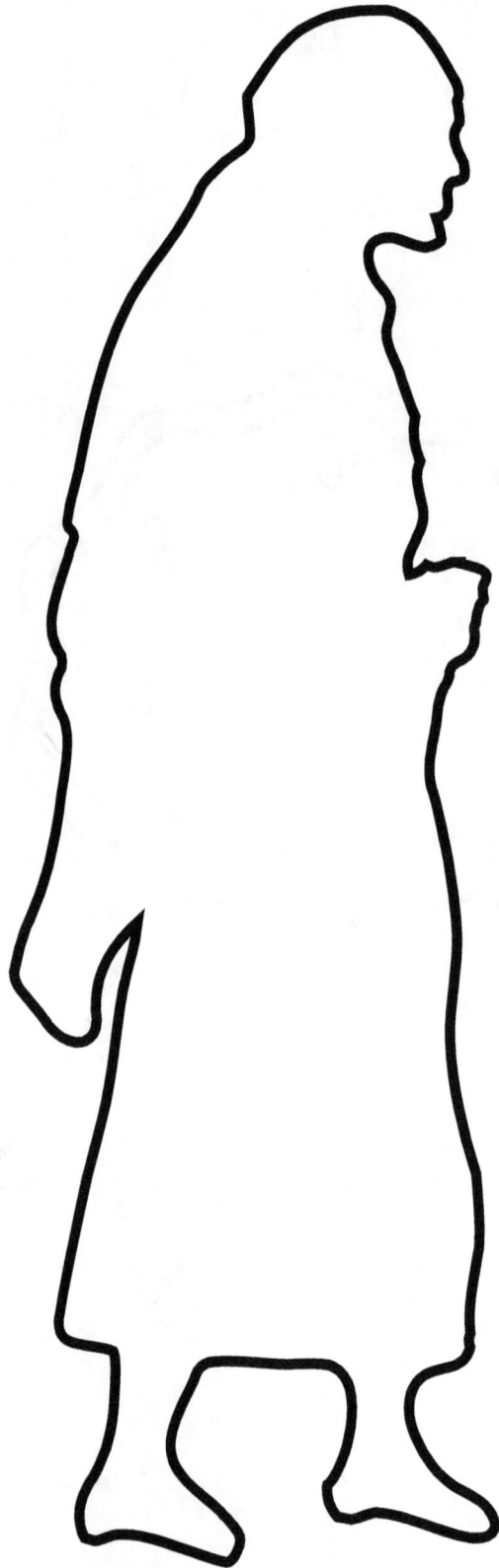

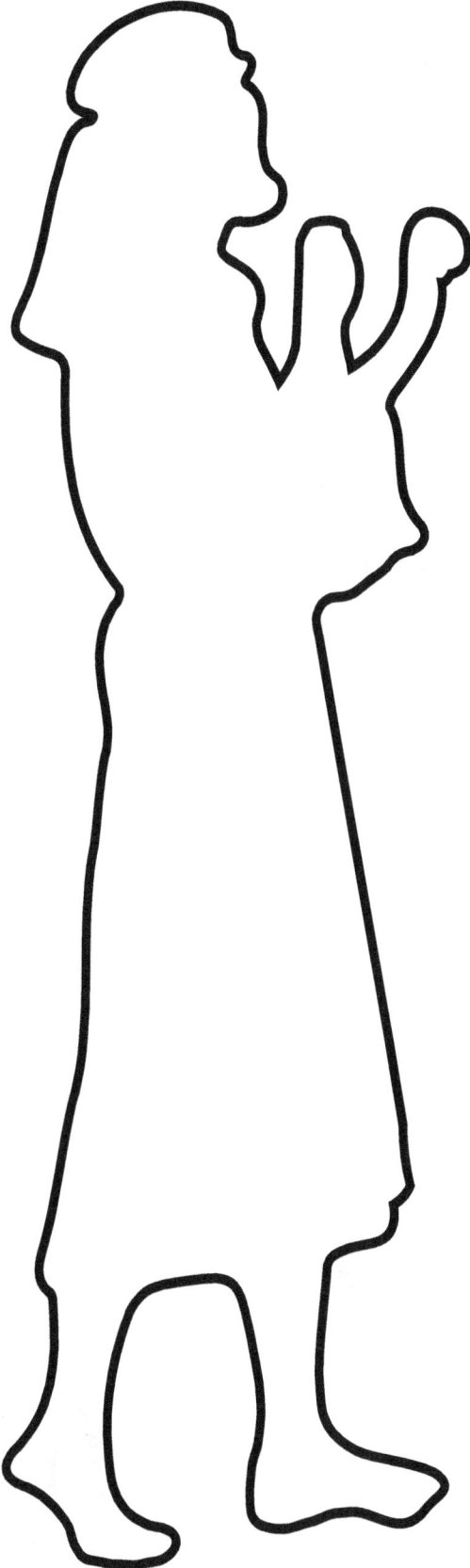

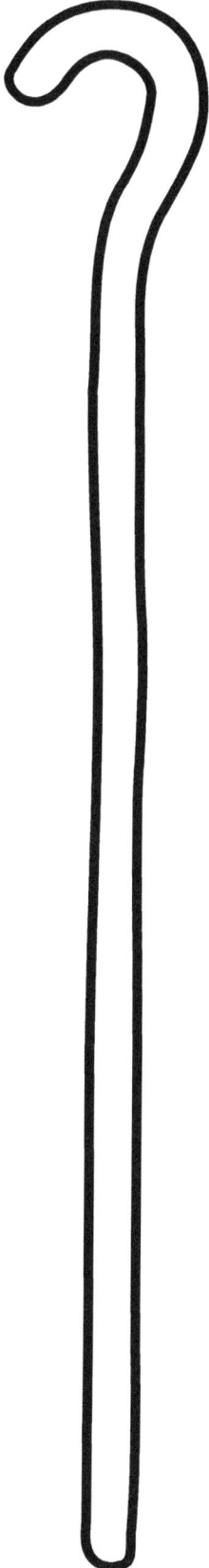

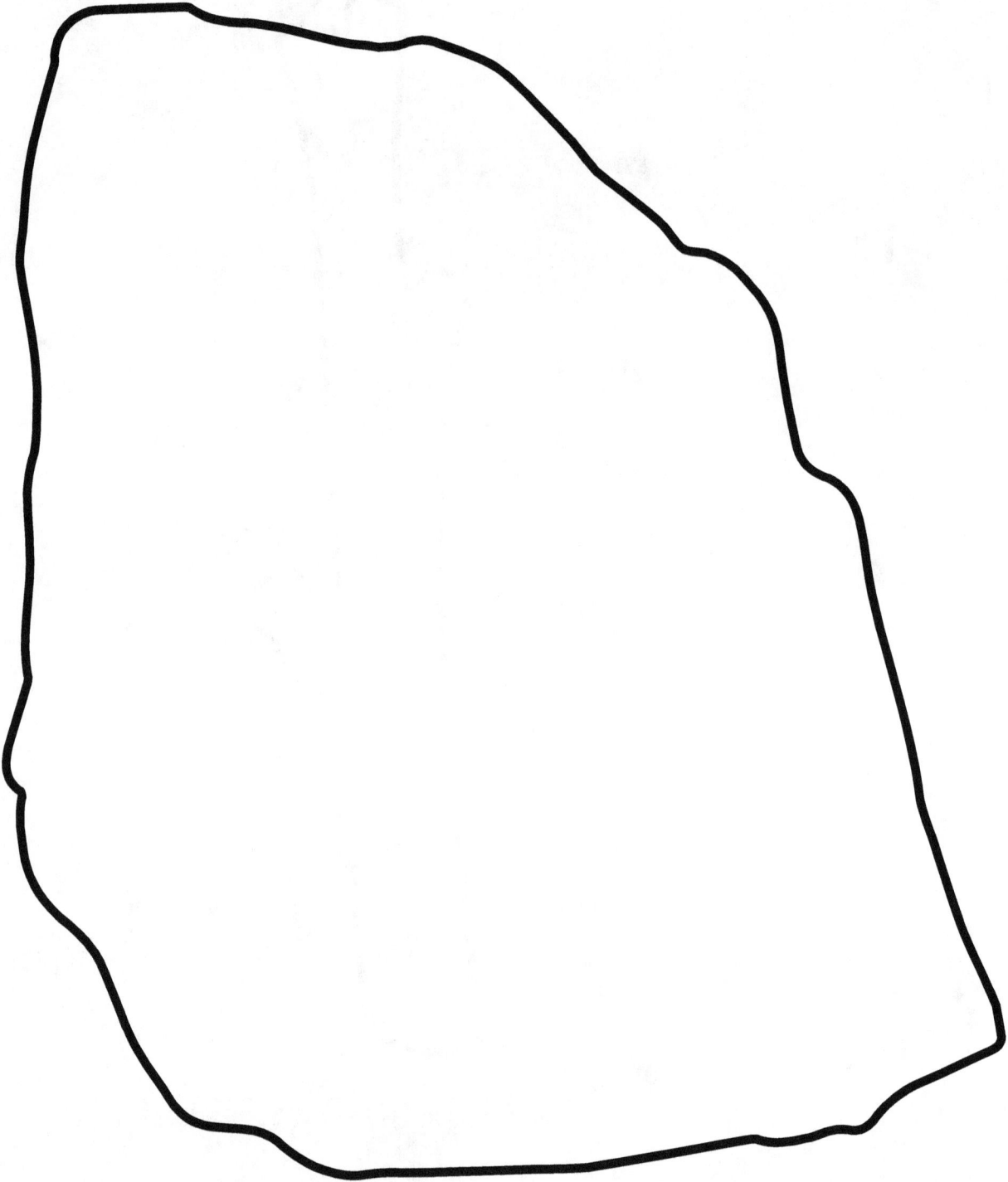

LESSON 4

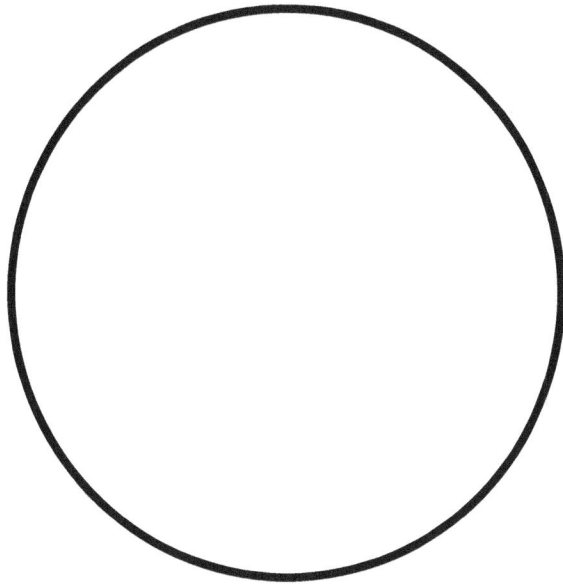

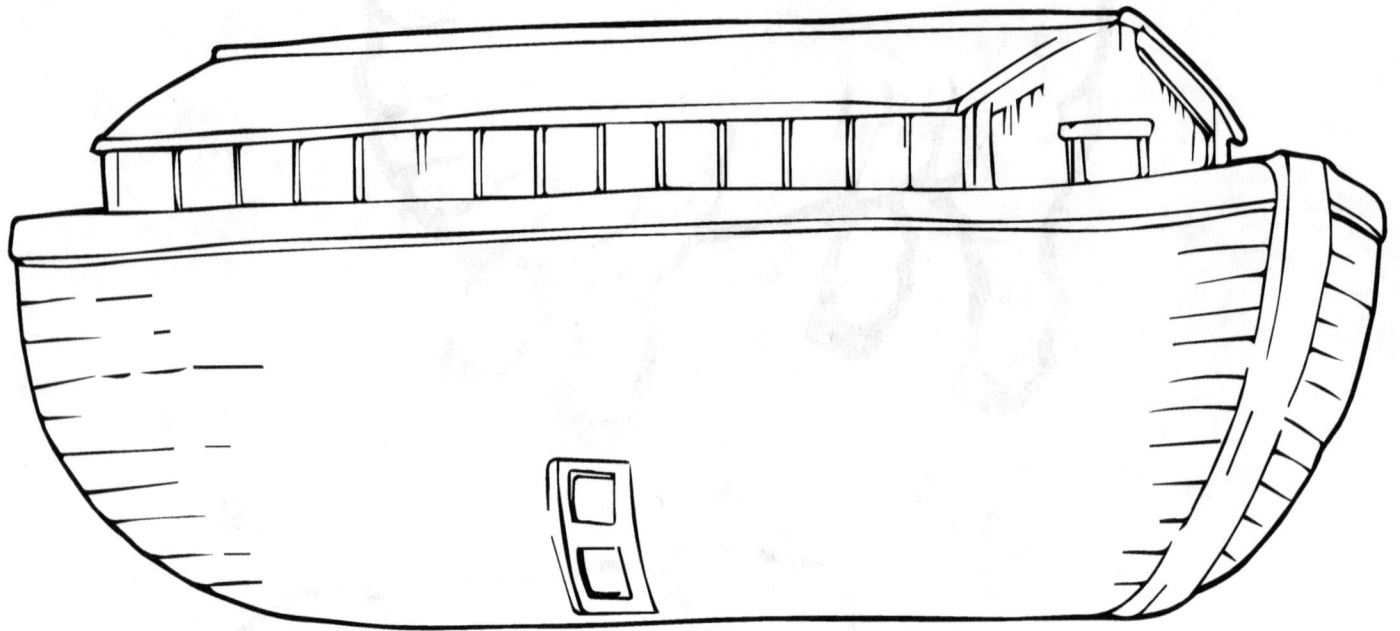

SOUL

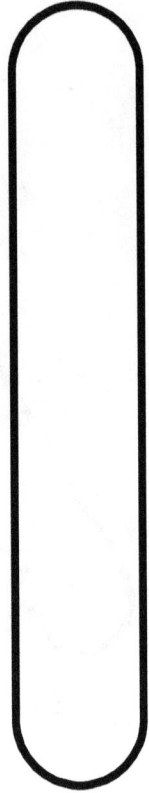

SPIRIT

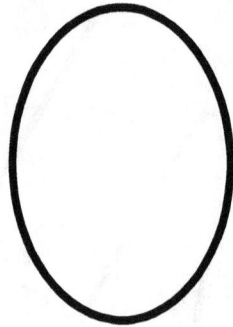

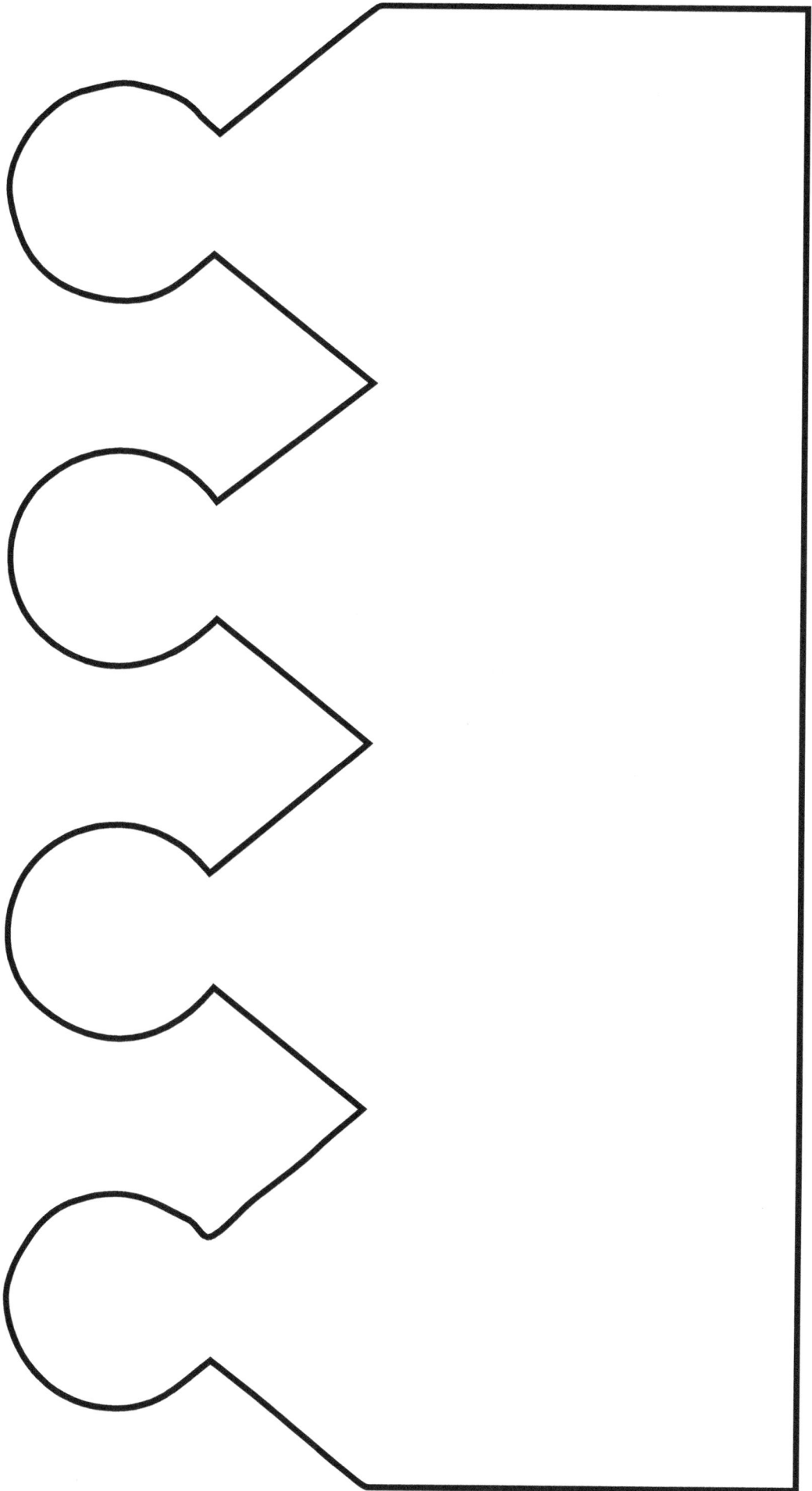

LESSON 8

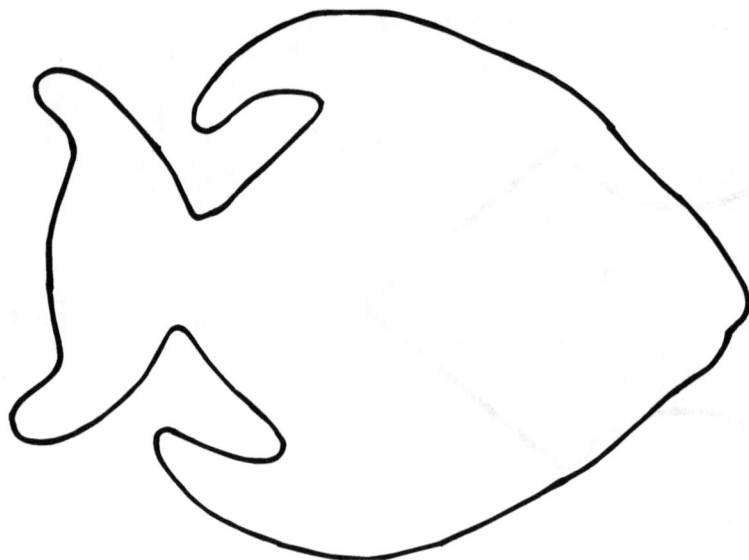